ABOUT THE AUTHOR

Ellen Gunning MA, MIAPR, FPRII, NUJ, is the director of the Irish Academy of Public Relations, which she formed in 1992. The Academy provides global online training in public relations, journalism, event management, radio and mobile journalism, social media marketing and grammar. It also offers radio and television presenting courses in Dublin. Academy courses are taught by forty partner colleges throughout Ireland and by colleges in Greece and Nigeria. It has just formed the first online academy in the Middle East – the Orient Planet Academy – which is a joint venture with Arab partners. In addition, the college has co-operation agreements with colleges and world trade centres in Chile, Uruguay, Paraguay and France.

Ellen has worked in PR and event management since the 1980s, and has handled some of the largest PR campaigns in the country, including The Kerrygold Dublin Horse Show, National Energy Awareness Week and a presidential campaign. She is the author of *Public Relations – A Practical Approach* (Gill & Macmillan 2003), the core text, nationwide, for all students studying public relations in Ireland. Her second book was *Capital Women of Influence* (Liffey Press, 2009).

Ellen has served as a government-appointed director to the boards of the National Concert Hall and the Central Council of the Irish Red Cross. She was a Forbairt mentor for a number of years, and is a former board member of the Public Relations Institute of Ireland. In January 2007 the Public Relations Institute of Ireland conferred her with a fellowship. In 2011 she won the European Parliament Broadcast Journalist of the Year award (Ireland).

A member of the Professional Speaking Association, Ellen regularly addresses SMEs at conferences, seminars and meetings about ways in which businesses can improve their profile and generate more publicity.

TEN
RED-HOT
TIPS
TO PROMOTE
YOUR BUSINESS

ELLEN GUNNING

MERCIER PRESS
IRISH PUBLISHER – IRISH STORY

MERCIER PRESS
Cork
www.mercierpress.ie

© Ellen Gunning, 2016

ISBN: 978 1 78117 410 4

10 9 8 7 6 5 4 3 2 1

A CIP record for this title is available from the British Library

Printed and bound in the EU.

CONTENTS

INTRODUCTION

If I was down to my last dollar, I'd spend it on public relations.

Bill Gates

I love quotes. They have a habit of encapsulating a huge amount of information in a sentence or two. In this one, Bill Gates, one of the most successful entrepreneurs in the world, says he would spend his last dollar on PR. Interesting, isn't it?

If your business, charity, organisation, sports group or club is not investing in public relations, what does Bill Gates know that you don't? When someone mentions Bill Gates, what is your first thought? You immediately associate him with Microsoft, don't you? After that, you think about a specific association, which could be about his life, the products his company makes, their ethics, their share price or their employment policies. You begin, however, with a knowledge of Bill Gates. Public relations creates that knowledge.

There is only one thing in the world worse than being talked about and that is not being talked about.

Oscar Wilde

I disagree with this quote in one sense, but I understand the essence of it. Public relations is about getting people to talk about you – your company, your brand, your product. Sales people will tell you that it is easy to sell something from a known producer and almost impossible to sell a product – no matter how good it is – if people have never heard of the company.

Think about it. Would you join a local club that no one in your area was aware of? Would you spend the same amount of money on a plate from an unknown company (no matter how good the quality) as you would on a Wedgwood plate? Of course not. In order to invest your time or your money you need to know more.

That's what PR does. It promotes your business to an audience of potential customers or influencers, and helps them to build up a store of knowledge that will ultimately make it easier for you to sell to them. People buy brands that they know and trust. The brand doesn't have to be an international one, but it needs to be known to its target audience.

Going back to the Oscar Wilde quote – remember that the talk about you could be negative too (shabby products, dismissive staff, late deliveries, over-priced goods, etc.). It's not always good, but, if your business is well run and you get the PR right, then you have nothing to fear.

PR is a combination of creative thinking, persistence,

knowledge of the market you are operating in (including the media and web markets) and devoting time to learning and applying the techniques. It needs time. Time to create the 'angles' that will interest the media. Time to work out the real cost of a sponsorship. Time to craft press releases. The return on investment, however, can be quite substantial.

PR techniques can be used by organisations of all sizes. What I will show you, in this book, is a range of PR techniques and how to use them. You won't apply all of the techniques – they won't all be relevant to your business – but the techniques you decide to use will enhance your presence in the market and generate talk about you, your business and your products. That makes it easier for you to sell. Sales create profits and profits allow you to grow your business, expand into new markets, create more employment and pursue other avenues of interest.

So, let's get started!

GROUND RULES

Let's establish the ground rules.

The reason you are reading this book is because you believe that using PR techniques will enhance your business, organisation, group or charity. Well done – you are on the road to success already.

Let me also assume that you lack sufficient budget to retain the services of a PR consultancy, or you are curious and want to find out what PR can actually do! Either way, you are looking to get the most useful, practical, up-to-date, innovative ideas and strategies that you can implement for yourself. You have come to the right place.

Finally, allow me to assume that you do not want to re-invent the wheel. You want to use tried and trusted strategies, and learn from the success of other small to medium-sized businesses that have used PR to enhance their presence in the market and generate more interest in their business. Terrific. You are the reader I am looking for.

By the end of this book I hope that you will have amassed plenty of techniques – some of which will apply to your business, some of which will not – but all of which will make you question what you do and the way that you do it. By the end of this book, you will have identified specific areas of PR that you can use for the benefit of your business.

Before you can use PR techniques you need to know what PR is capable of doing. Let's start by looking at what it cannot do.

Ground rule number one is that PR is not a substitute for advertising.

Advertising creates an opportunity for you to sell a specific product to a specific audience at a specific price. If you are buying advertising space, you are doing so because the media you are buying it in is the right one for your audience. So if you know that most people who use your product will search for it online, you might use Google or Facebook advertising; or if you know that the people who buy your product read the *Sunday Independent*, you could buy space in that medium to advertise. Alternatively research might have told you that your potential customers prefer a visual medium and can be reached by television (and there has been an explosion in TV channels available to you if you are looking to advertise).

In advertising, you target a specific audience, pay by column-inch or pay per click or amount of airtime, and evaluate the success by the volume of sales you achieve. Simple.

Rule number two is that you must know who you are trying to influence.

PR is all about communication. It's about communicating with people who are relevant to your business. If you produce a product or service, you know exactly who your potential purchaser is. PR tools will help you find ways to reach that potential purchaser.

So you need to know what audience you are targeting. A good example is a west Cork-based jeweller who briefed the Irish Academy of Public Relations some years ago. The jeweller made hand-crafted, exquisite, expensive jewellery, which retailed from a small shop in west Cork. She wanted to increase her business by creating greater awareness of her shop. I asked her if she could describe a typical purchaser: 'Who buys your product?' This woman really knew her business, so she answered, 'The people who buy my jewellery are in their mid-thirties. They are professional couples mostly, both working, with two children. They live in south county Dublin but have a holiday home in west Cork. They usually drive a four-by-four, spend about three days at a time in their holiday home and buy on impulse when they are in town. They are cash rich, time poor and indulge themselves and their children. They have plenty of money but very little time.'

I was in hog-heaven!! With this type of description I could go away and figure out what these people read, watched, listened to and browsed, and so could start to make it easy for them to find the jeweller in the media places that they frequented.

Rule number three is target your audience.

Stop trying to change your customers to make them more like you! It's not about you, it's about the people who buy from you. Don't try to inform people through the media that you prefer. Instead, find the media that your customers and potential customers frequent and inform them there. Bring the mountain to Muhammad.

If most of your clients read *The Irish Sun* and the *Sunday World*, there's absolutely no point in you getting publicity in *The Irish Times* and *The Sunday Business Post*. That would simply be vanity coverage. Your colleagues in business, your neighbours, people at the golf club will see the piece and comment on it to you. But if they don't buy from you, or influence people who buy from you, you are wasting your time, effort and energy (and these are all limited resources). Act wisely – know the people you are trying to target.

Rule number four is research.

You need to do research to find out what is of interest to your audience. Things which interest people in their mid-thirties are very different to the interests of people in their mid-sixties, and differ again from a mid-teens audience. Data really is king. So, if you are targeting people in their mid-sixties, what kind of people are you seeking? You might be looking for people who are cash rich, at a bit of a loose end and likely to avail of your exclusive travel opportunities. You might be looking, alternatively, for people in their mid-sixties who are cash poor but are time rich and have devoted a lifetime to rearing their families and providing for them, without ever devoting any time to themselves. Your market might be people who want a bit of adventure but at a reasonable cost (think bus tours instead of Caribbean cruises). Your mid-sixties people might not be either rich or poor but might, instead, have a common interest. You might be specifically targeting opera-lovers, or readers of Shakespeare, or people who love the movies and want to visit different film locations. You cannot put everyone into a single category to target them. That is the equivalent of using a splurge-gun. In PR we like to use a bow and arrow!

The fastest and most cost-effective way to do this type of research – always – is to ask your existing customers. You can do this verbally when they call into your shop, by online survey, or by calling them to chat on the phone. You can select the age range (from your existing database) and they can give you valuable insights into the reasons why they chose your company, a particular product, etc.

Rule number five is identify the trends.

What is 'trending' among that audience? What's cool and what's not? Think cooking for a moment. Years ago everyone was slow-cooking. You couldn't turn sideways but someone was talking about it. It was the hot trend of the time and if you were promoting a food product, you needed to tie it into the slow-food movement. Yet I haven't heard it mentioned in quite a while. Instead, for quite a few years now it has been all about 'organic' food. We are all trying to buy the best-quality produce so that we can produce the healthiest meals.

Nowadays we are into lifestyle, health and food knowledge. Think McDonalds. Everyone associates the company with a Big Mac and fries (at least everyone I know does!). They are known and loved for it all over the world. But a few years ago people started talking about how unhealthy burgers and chips were, how overeating was causing diabetes and obesity in children, how eating too many Big Macs was bad for you. Now, common sense tells you that eating too much of anything is bad for you, and a Big Mac and fries is perfectly fine as a treat. But McDonalds were aware that the publicity was doing them damage, so they introduced the McDonald's salad range. I have no idea how many people eat salads in McDonalds, and I have no idea (when you calculate the dressings, croutons etc.) if they are, in fact any healthier than the burger option. What I do know is that it doesn't really matter. From McDonald's point of view they needed to change the conversation. They had to stop people talking about 'unhealthy' in the same breath as McDonalds. The salad range allowed that to happen. In fact, people just stopped talking about McDonalds, which was good, and, I presume, just went back to eating there. The company reacted to the trend, preserved their market share and kept their customers happy.

You can spend a fortune doing research and, if you have money to spend, it is always a good way to spend it. However, as a small business, you are probably best doing a Google search (put in plenty of questions about the same topic and you'll get a good overview from the information that Google presents) and chat with colleagues, friends and family. Often we are not even aware that we are noticing trends. Chatting to people reminds them – and you – of what you are already aware of but didn't compute for your business.

Rule number six is look at your customers' media habits.
Now that you know the audience and what is trending with them, your next step is to find out what media they read. Don't make the mistake of thinking that media is entirely age-related. It is not, although age can be a good guide. Some people like to get all their information from printed

newspapers, while others only read them occasionally. For example, there are those who read a newspaper (or more) every day, while others only buy newspapers on the day that the property supplement or agricultural supplement, for instance, appears. For others, a daily paper is not of interest, but their Sunday revolves around taking a couple of hours to sit and review the week's events through the columns of their favourite newspaper.

For some industries, magazines are still hugely important. Think fashion and beauty, for example. It's hard to imagine how these industries would survive without magazines deliberately (advertising) or subtly (through PR) promoting the latest trends, colours, fabrics – and all associated with celebrity. (This also happens on television.)

In contrast, nowadays, for many, information comes online, in the form of RSS feeds, Facebook, constant visits to favourite media websites, tweets or newspapers' daily online 'bulletins'. For these people, the depth of information is less important than the speed. They want to know immediately if something has happened and they will then choose which online medium to visit to get more information. Their online feeds may also send them in the direction of radio or TV coverage for more detail.

Some people get most of their information from the radio – I'm one of those! I am a radio junkie. I travel quite a bit and love listening to the radio when I'm in the car.

I will listen to any daytime talk show that is debating an issue of even mild interest to me. (I cannot bear listening to the night-time shock jocks, and instantly switch channels when anything sports-related is debated.) Most of the current affairs information that I gain is through radio so, if I were your target, radio would definitely be the best way to reach me.

Finally, people still get information from television, although it is no longer consumed in the way that it was. While I've read that less than 30 per cent of people watch pre-recorded shows, my circle of friends and acquaintances would reflect my own TV experiences – I watch 70 per cent pre-recorded and about 30 per cent live. Lifestyle dictates more and more that people watch programmes when it suits them, but they also watch on mobile devices. The number of people watching television on a screen on a wall in a room in their home is declining rapidly! The trend nowadays is that people watch TV while texting on their mobiles, or tweeting about what they are watching (or tweeting the programme if it is live) and/or checking their Facebook pages. People use multiple devices at the one time. It is much more difficult nowadays to get someone's full and undivided attention.

With so many different media available it is more important than ever to target the right ones for your intended customers.

The final rule is find out who they admire and follow.
When you have a good handle on the people you are trying to reach (PR people call them publics) you need to start finding out who influences them. Is it politicians, business people, movie stars, sporting heroes, musicians or celebrities? After that, you need to find out exactly which politicians (Leo Varadkar or Hilary Clinton), and so on.

Only with all this knowledge accumulated are you ready to start work.

PR creates knowledge, empathy, understanding and interest. It tells you about the business, who is behind it, how it has grown over the years, how many people it employs and if it is good to its employees and the environment. It creates a mental picture in the mind of the purchaser that makes it easier for the advertising people. If the purchaser already knows something about the company, then, when someone approaches them to buy the product, they begin by thinking 'I've heard of them', or 'they are that new company in Cork'. This makes it easier for the advertising person to sell the product.

You need to set clear objectives for your PR activities. What are you trying to achieve with the publicity you will get? If you don't set objectives at the start, you have no hope of achieving them, or being able to quantify what return you got for all your effort.

PR is good at creating name awareness. People buy brands. If they haven't heard of you, it is much more difficult to sell to them. So name awareness is important for any brand or company. But you might have other reasons for wanting to raise your profile. You might be introducing a new range of products, which are substantially different to those you are traditionally known for. This means that you need to prime the market in advance of the new product launch to expect this new stream of products from you. That is a good reason for generating publicity. Or it might be something as simple as the fact that your competitors have started appearing everywhere and your company does not have a profile. People will start to think of your competitors first and may not be conscious that there is an alternative – your business. That is a good reason for getting involved in PR.

Often companies do good things – they sponsor events in their local community, or voluntarily introduce structures that are kind to the environment, or are involved in things that would be regarded as good citizenship or corporately responsible behaviour. You might want to earn credit for these endeavours. After all, you are not obliged to give anything back, you are doing that because you care and your clients – and competitors – should know about it!

It is important to do some research in the early stages. You want more people to know about your business.

Excellent. How many people know about you right now in your locality? Nationally? In your industry? The answer for each will probably be different. You might be very well-known within your own industry, but hardly known at all to a national audience. If you can conduct some research at the start, to establish the true situation, your goals will be more realistic and the evaluation of your success will be more realistic too. For example, if 5 per cent of the local community can name your company, unprompted, in a survey of producers of your particular type of product, then, depending on your budget, it might be reasonable to seek to increase that to 20 per cent by the end of the year. You will also, of course, need to conduct research to establish if you have reached your targets.

Now you need to write a plan. Things don't just happen. They happen because you plan them. You need to plan clearly if you are doing PR internally. Remember that PR is very time-consuming, so you need to allow time to write press releases, organise functions, generate photo calls, etc. Planning will also allow you to identify the stories that you want to tell people – you might organise a Christmas party for senior citizens each year (there's a story and a photo opportunity right there), you might know that you will be launching a new product next March (plan to maximise publicity at that time) and you might know that you will be speaking at a major conference in September.

Those three items could be more than enough for the first year.

Planning means creating a timeline, but it also involves allocating a budget to your activities. You may not be paying an hourly fee to a PR consultancy, but you will still need a budget for photos (the photographer, models, costumes, etc.), or functions (food and drink, room hire, MC), or exhibitions (leaflets, backdrops, competitions, prizes), to make them happen.

Your plan will also include the media you are targeting, the stories you need to research, the people you need to get quotes from, the photographers you propose to use, etc. It will identify the tools you propose to use – photo calls, press conferences, exhibitions, conferences, seminars, third-party endorsement, press receptions, ezines, social media – and how much time and focus you will devote to each. You cannot leave anything to chance. Meticulous planning is one of the hallmarks of good professional PR.

If properly written, your plan will also include how to evaluate your success at the end of the year. What additional research will you need so that you know you reached your goal? Can you show that you got coverage in your target media (and not just in 'the media' generally)? Have you any feedback to indicate what people thought of the coverage? How many people had an opportunity to see it? Have your enquiries increased? Do people speak about you differently? Do they recognise the company name when you introduce yourself? Look at things like viewership statistics and readership numbers to calculate how many people had an opportunity to see the coverage. Build in a 'where did you hear about us' box on your enquiry forms (online and offline). Get staff into the habit of noting what people said about the company – 'a friend suggested I call you/I was searching on Google the other night and your company came up/I was just passing and saw your display'. These are all very useful evaluation tools.

The evaluation of your first year, which should be done on a monthly basis, but should also be done at the end of the year looking back over twelve months, will help to guide you going forward. You should be learning about what does and doesn't work for your business, what proved to be too time-consuming (even if it was a good idea), or what you did not get a return on (the photo call that no one used photos from). Crucially, you should be learning how to do things smarter and better for the next year.

Think carefully about the positives – and negatives – of attracting media publicity. The media seldom come looking for you (unless there is a crisis). You are the one who raises your head above the parapet and says, 'Look at me. My business is wonderful. Let's tell the world about us.' By doing so, you also give the media permission to look closely at your business and find fault, expose bad practice, and complain that you do not deliver what you promise. It's a two-way street. Before you go public at all, make sure that everything you do will stand up to public scrutiny.

There is one final thing to tell you. It is not something that people necessarily associate with the PR industry and it is to the shame of the industry that they have never addressed the issue – *always be truthful*. You do not have to tell all of the truth all of the time. No one does. There is no reason why people should think of your business as an open book any more than they should think of you, personally, as an open book. There is nothing wrong with showing your best side in public. We all do that when we get dressed each morning – we decide what image we will project for that day. And there is nothing wrong with answering a question truthfully but without detail. Indeed, it is not always possible to give all of the detail, for example, because of stock exchange rules, or ongoing investigation, or common humanity, or fear of litigation. There are many valid reasons why businesses cannot answer questions fully. However, that is a world away from telling lies.

People think that PR is about telling lies and being clever about how you tell them. Wrong. If you tell lies, you'll be found out. If you are found out, people won't trust you. If they don't trust you, they won't buy from you. If they don't buy from you, you don't have a business. Warren Buffet, one of the USA's best-known investors, cautioned: 'It takes twenty years to build a reputation and five minutes to ruin it. If you think about that, you will do things differently.'

PR is about building your reputation. Don't build a shoddy one.

1

PRESS RELEASES

Writing a press release is the most basic thing that a PR person can do and it's something you should be able to do as well. It's not rocket science. There is a structure to how a press release is written, what information it should contain, who you should send it to, etc. So let me tell you how the professionals do it.

First we need to establish what a press release actually is. My definition is that a press release is information, written in a journalistic style, which would be of interest to the readers/listeners or viewers of a particular medium. In other words, if a newspaper had sent a reporter, this is the way they would have written the story for their readers. News editors will advise you, if you are an SME, to select someone from the business and get them trained in how to write press releases.

A press release is not information that you would like people to know about you. It should be information that they would find interesting. For example, you might want people to know that your business is well run, you have survived the recent downturn and business is now picking up again. This is important information for you and your employees but, honestly, it is of no interest to the general public and, therefore, of no interest to a journalist. Or if you were offering 10 per cent off the price of your product for the next fortnight, this is something that you would want people to know, but a journalist would not regard it as news. That is advertising. Buy space in the newspaper and sell to people. If you are introducing a new range of shoes, for example, into your shop … well, now you are getting closer. But you still don't have a press release. You have found a fact – always important in every story – now you need to build up more information to flesh it out.

A press release must have an interesting angle. A reader might have no interest in the fact that you are producing a new bath mat, but they might be curious about the fact that this non-slip mat was created as a result of a bad fall that the father of the owner had when he was getting out of the bath. They might further be interested in the fact that this clever little idea will create five more jobs in a company that currently employs ten people. That's a massive increase in employment in one small business. The reader might also be curious about the fact that this bath mat will replace a non-slip product which is currently being imported, thereby giving people a chance to buy Irish at the same price and quality.

The first question you should ask yourself, when issuing a press release, is would people be interested in reading about this? You need to have the ability to honestly say 'no they wouldn't' and start again. It is difficult for most small businesses to identify the newsworthy element of a story. Everything that your business does is of huge interest to you – and rightly so. It is your business. You are proud of every achievement and want to shout about it from the rooftops. But Joe and Josephine public do not share your enthusiasm. If you are trying to influence them, you need to find an angle that will encourage them to read.

Once complete, a press release is sent to a journalist or news desk in a particular paper. The job of the person at the other end is to determine whether or not their readers would be interested in this information. Your job is to make sure that their answer is 'yes'.

Try not to be too corporate. For example, a company called Magoo Travel sends out a press release stating in the top line that the price of flights to Las Vegas has been cut to €1,200 and then goes on to explain what a super deal this is. Buried in the middle of the release is a mention that sales of flights to Las Vegas have recovered by 15 per cent since last year – this is the real story. The way to tell it would have been to start with the information that Magoo Travel has noticed a 15 per cent increase in flights to Las Vegas. The rest of the story might be about why there is an increase in exotic holidays, or if this is a symptom of desperation and that people are going gambling, or a sign that the dollar is weak. The end of the release might give details of the special offer. Try to think like a journalist and find the angle to a story – what would make it newsworthy? Is it information which is of value to the reader?

You may not immediately have enough information to go with your angle. If you are a local shoe shop, for example, and you have just started stocking a new brand of shoes, that is an interesting fact – but it is not enough for a press release. The angle is in the 'why' – why have you suddenly started stocking them? It might be that there has been a change in buying patterns, and you will need to get statistics out of your own business and possibly from other sources to show that people are buying fewer but better quality shoes. On further investigation you might find that this is because, in recessionary times, people want their shoes to last longer. Or you might be stocking the new brand because there has been an upturn in the market and you have found that people are starting to look, once again, for shoes that are a bit more glamorous. They are no longer looking for good, hard-wearing shoes (which have been your stock in trade throughout the recession) but are now coming into your store looking for something more stylish. It might be that heel heights have changed, or that there is a new walking club in your area and everyone is buying walking shoes. The story (the 'why') is what will interest the reader. An advertisement would tell them that new Brand X shoes are in stock. A press release will tell them about changing trends in footwear that your shop has identified. As a consequence of reading about it, the reader will know that your shoe shop carries that particular range.

If you need to create the information for the angle, you will probably have to do some research. It does not have to be expensive, and it can be very effective. People love statistics: the top ten reasons why people change their cars, the five 'must have' colours for this season, the four things that every classy bathroom has, the six best colleges to study at, etc. Statistics attract the attention of the journalist and the reader.

Now that you have an angle, you need to start preparing the press release. A press release should always answer six questions, known as the 5Ws and H: who, where, what, when, why and how. All six should be answered in the first two paragraphs of your release, although not necessarily in that order.

If, for example, you have someone famous opening your new premises, then the *who* might be very important. Readers will want to know that a famous model, or the lord mayor or a well-known GAA player performed the opening. If, however, the managing director of your company, who is not a well-known national figure, did the opening, you might not use this information until further down the body of the release.

The *where* is important if you are issuing to a local newspaper. The *Southside People* will want to know that something happened in Dún Laoghaire, but if it happened in Howth, on the north side of Dublin, you might not use the information prominently in your release.

What is sometimes overlooked in the rush to create a press release. What is happening? A new premises being opened? A new product launched? A new charity created which will raise funds for children with cancer? A report published which shows that people are marrying later in life? A bank announcing that it has increased lending to SMEs? It is important to make clear what the focus of the release is.

When is vital. No one wants to be receiving old or stale news. Always include *when* something happened in your press release. This guarantees the reader (in this case the journalist) that the information is fresh and you are not simply rehashing an old press release that wasn't picked up by the media first time around. This is the reason why you never use words like 'recently' in a press release. 'Recently' could mean that it happened this morning, but it might also mean that it happened last month. Always give the dates in brackets in the body of the release, as a reassurance to the journalists who are reading it (they will delete the date from the text when it appears in the newspaper).

Why and *how* are the two questions that add meat to the bones of the release. *Why* has the company moved premises? Why is there a need for another children's cancer charity? Why has a report on marriage habits been issued now? Why is the bank increasing its lending to SMEs? And *how* did it all come about? How will this charity differ from others? How will the move to bigger premises secure the employment of people within the business? How will later marriages affect the birth rate in the future? And remember that *how* can also mean *how much*? How much does the charity hope to raise? How much money is the bank making available? How much did the business move cost? Business media, in particular, always look for figures – money, jobs created, turnover, investment, percentage increase in sales, etc.

The other reason for issuing a press release is a major crisis situation in a business. In this instance a press release acts as a holding mechanism until you can make yourself available at a press conference. If you are issuing a press release for this reason, the *why* and *how* questions are usually the most difficult to answer. How was this tragedy allowed to happen? Why did no one do something about safety at the company before it became a crisis? Why did no one in authority feel that there was a need to act on this issue before now? How did no one notice that money was going missing? Why were better checks not in place? How did it get to the stage where someone had to go public in order to have their complaint heard and properly dealt with?

The *why* and *how* can be tricky in a crisis (but they still need to be answered). In this type of situation, if you are the one answering these questions you are already in trouble. The questions are generated because of curiosity or anger, so the person answering is inevitably on the back foot. You are defending a position, which is always a weak starting point.

No matter what the reason is for its creation, a press release is always written in the style of an inverted pyramid. The most important information goes at the top and the least important goes at the bottom. Newspapers cut information from the bottom up, so that the information for publication will fit on the page. They assume that the most important information is given first. After all, a press release is news and we are used to getting our news in short, sharp bites.

Your press release should always have a title that tells the journalist or news editor what they are going to read about. When the press release arrives into a media inbox, the subject line (your title) determines whether or not

it will be read. It is not your job to create a headline –
someone in the paper will do that. Your job is to 'flag' the
contents: Company Announces Thirteen New Jobs/New
Children's Charity Launched in Dublin, etc. The headline
writer will then create the newspaper headline, which
might be 'Company Announces Employment for Baker's
Dozen' or 'Suffer Little Children?'

Your release also needs to be dated. This is less important now that inboxes automatically show the date on
which something was received, but it is still used by most
people issuing releases. The top left of the page says Press
Release or Media Release and the top right gives the date
of issue. This is followed by the title and then the text of
the release.

A press release must use simple language. The purpose
of the release is to impart knowledge and information.
If you blind people with technical terms, use very long
words and seek to portray yourself as a terribly intelligent
person, you've missed the point. It should be capable
of being read and understood by a seven-year-old. No
fancy words. No flowery language. No hyperbole. Just
plain, simple language. If you explain something clearly
there is less opportunity for people to misinterpret or
misunderstand what you are saying. You also create less
work for the journalist when the release is received. They
get thousands of press releases every day. If they have to

change words, sentences and phrases in your release, then you are, quite simply, too much trouble. It is far easier to delete yours and look for another one. Cruel but true. No one has time to correct what you have written. Write in the style that the papers use and you have a much better chance of being covered.

Using simple language also means being careful not to use industry expressions which people don't understand. You can say that all of the bulbs you use in the hotel are CFLs but you need to explain that CFL means Compact Fluorescent Light and indicates that these are long-life bulbs. Make it simple. If people don't understand, they will move on from your story to another and your chance to inform them is lost.

You should also use short sentences. Long sentences do not work well either in a print format or on a website. Think about it. Newspaper columns are long and narrow. The shorter the words, the more likely they are to fit within the width of a column. The shorter the sentences, the more likely you are to fit three or four into a newspaper paragraph. Long sentences may be set as entire paragraphs, which makes reading them much more difficult. (The sensation of reading across narrow columns is very different to that of reading across a page. Longer sentences work well in letters, books and feature articles.)

Be careful about the words you use. People can take

offence at almost anything nowadays, and the last thing you want to do is generate debate about the word you used instead of the point you were trying to make. We live in an increasingly PC society – be sure that you proof-read your text with that in mind. Businesswoman will cause offence, businessperson will not. Follicly challenged may bring a wry smile to your face – but it won't insult bald people. Doormen become ushers, waitresses become waiting staff, etc.

Let us also deal with *spin*. Many PR people get very upset when you accuse them of spinning. When I was introduced by a colleague as 'the mistress of the dark art of spinning', I took it as a supreme compliment! Everyone spins. Not one of us tells all of the truth, all of the time. Not one of us believes that people are entitled to know everything about us. Most of us will dodge questions like: what age are you, or, what weight are you? And we are allowed to do so. We develop clever answers to questions that we do not want to answer. What age are you? – 'Well now, I'm older than I was last year but younger than I'll be next year. Sure none of us is getting any younger.' What weight are you? 'I'm probably not my ideal weight but I honestly don't know as I banned weighing scales from my home about ten years ago. I feel as if I am the right weight – and that's what's important to me.' You're not telling lies. But you're not answering the question either!

Businesses are the same. Spinning is not lying, it is putting the focus somewhere else. Spin is creating a story around the fact that you have lost weight without saying that you have another stone to lose before you reach your proper weight. Spinning is putting your best foot forward and focusing on the positive. Companies work hard to provide 'secure employment' for their workforce, which may also involve making people redundant due to changing commercial circumstances. They don't focus on letting people go, they focus on the jobs that have been secured as a result. That is spinning. It is perfectly true. It is not denying that redundancies have happened, it is not changing the number of people who lost their jobs, or how horrific the situation is for those workers and for the workers who remain, but it is very definitely pointing to the positive outcomes which result from these moves. We all do it. Spin is good provided it is truthful.

Ideally you are going to write four paragraphs of information for your press release. If you write more, you need to go back and edit and re-craft your story (or you need to tell it in a different way). Too much information might indicate that the story would be better told in a feature interview or on radio. It might also indicate that you are packing too much 'padding' into the release. 'Padding' is information about when the company was formed, what a good job it is doing, how the named director is 'director of marketing in Ireland and Europe with special responsibility for developing new markets in Asia minor and Russia'. The only reason you would refer to the company's age is if it was very new or very old, and 'doing a good job' could suggest that you had not always done so! And the marketing director's full title is probably not relevant to the press release – chances are that only one of the regions for which they have responsibility is relevant to the story, so you can leave out the rest.

The release always closes with the name of the person who should be contacted for further information, their phone number and the name of the organisation that the release was issued on behalf of (you won't need this element if you are issuing for your own business). But your release will always end: 'Further details: *Ellen Gunning, phone 081–2345678*'.

It sounds obvious, but remember to have your phone with you, and 'live', if you have a release out. People in the media do not work from 9 a.m. to 5 p.m. They may call you late in the evening to get more information, or to arrange an interview on an early morning radio programme. You want the publicity. It is your job to be sure that you are available. If you will not be in a position to answer your phone, give someone else's contact details. The media will not keep ringing you until you are ready or available to answer!

Once the release is ready it is important to make sure that you target the right journalists. Let me give you an example. I present the Mediascope programme on 103.2 Dublin City fm every Tuesday from early October to the end of June each year. My inbox is always jammed with press releases but many of them are deleted on sight. My programme deals with items of interest to people in the public relations, event management and journalism industries. Press release titles about new businesses being created, some team winning a prize, a new play opening in a theatre in town, etc., will not be read. They are not relevant to my audience. The release may be perfectly well written and very interesting to another radio show but it has been sent to the wrong person and it is not my job to re-direct it. I just bin it. Every journalist does the same. So, when you go to so much trouble to create a release, make sure that you send it to the right person.

You could, of course, take the same subject matter and make it relevant to my programme. Those same releases would be read if the subject lines read 'New Direct Marketing company opens', 'Winning team got 25k sponsorship to fund training', or 'New play looks at how the banking crash was communicated to the public'. See what I mean?

When you are issuing a release, compile a list of the media who would be interested in receiving it. If your business prints textbooks, then your media list will include all of the education correspondents, possibly book reviewers (depending on the topic) and specialist education magazines. You might also send your release to education programmes on radio and television. Don't forget bloggers – they are highly influential. Your release might also go up on your own website (if you don't have an area for media you should consider creating one), you might mention it on Twitter, and you might put a link and a visual on your Facebook page.

You should also remember that the purpose of the release is to attract media attention, so give the media a chance to cover the story. We arranged an event some years ago for a new service. The service was difficult to explain so we spent a lot of money creating something 'visual' to accompany the story. We also booked a guest speaker for the launch. On arrival, the guest cooed over our special creation and promptly photographed it and tweeted it to her thousands of followers before the event had even started! Please, exercise caution around the information and how it is issued. Don't (as happened on that occasion) allow yourself to be shot in the foot.

Once you have gone to all this trouble, creating angles, researching further information, possibly organising photographs to go with it, you have worked up a good media release. Now it is ready for issue. Here's how to do it.

While you can attach the release to an email, this is not advisable. Many of the national newspapers have computer systems which strip out attachments, and those that get through may not be read. Be sure to copy and paste your press release into the body of the email. Make sure that your subject line says 'Press Release:' followed by your heading, for example 'New Charity for Children with Cancer', so that the media know that it is information which they may freely use.

Remember, you might have spent hours or even days preparing the release, but it is issued free of charge to the media and they may choose to cover it, or not. You have no control over that. All you can reasonably hope to achieve is the best possible angle to the story, issued to the right media at the right time.

Timing is important. There is no point in issuing a release late on Tuesday night when the function is over. It is far better to issue the release early on Tuesday morning, written in the past tense with the time as well as the date included. You are aiming for coverage in Wednesday's paper so you need to give them adequate notice. Your release might say 'A new charity for children was launched by the Taoiseach yesterday (Tues x/x/2016 at 4.30 p.m.).'

Target your release. As I mentioned earlier, if you want to have the best chance of coverage, make sure that the release is relevant to the particular journalist. Emphasise the local angle to local media, the national angle to the nationals. Send an audio clip to radio stations with the press release, or offer someone for interview. Send a video clip to radio and TV as well as online media. Online media are always looking for video footage – radio and TV stations might not broadcast it but might use it online.

And what about following up? Generally it drives the media crazy to get a phone call asking if a release was received. What's the point? If you didn't think that your email was up to the job, you should have sent the information some other way! You can, occasionally, phone a journalist in advance to tell them that a press release will be sent to them later in the day and let them know what it is about. Don't get a junior to do this. The journalist may ask questions and there is nothing more infuriating than hooking the journalist's interest only to have someone tell them: 'I don't know. I'll get someone to call you back.' Very silly. It's like having a fish on the line and telling it: 'I have to go home for my tea now. I'll leave you free to swim around for another while and then I'll come back and try to hook you again.' We all move on very quickly!

So advance calls need to be done by someone with information about the item, and follow-up calls are similar. Follow-up calls, if you are making them, should be to give additional information, or to find out if another angle is of interest. This might be the case if, for example, you issued your press release to all media on Tuesday, but were still hoping for coverage in the Sunday papers and decided to phone those journalists on Thursday to see if you could interest them in further information. Don't twist arms, look for a favour, or seek publicity for anything other than the story. It diminishes you in the eyes of the journalist and confirms that the press release did not contain an interesting story in the first place!

I once received a press release that came by email with the following subject line: 'Please, please, would you do this interview?' The opening paragraph explained that the PR person's client had not been interviewed by anyone and she was desperate to get him some kind of coverage. Could I oblige? I honestly didn't know whether to laugh or cry. No one else in the world wanted to talk to this guy. How did I get so lucky? Needless to say, I didn't interview him.

If your press release is not covered – move on. No journalist is under obligation to cover your story, but equally they have not decided to put you on a list of people they will never cover. Your next release might be of more interest, or the one after that. In the early stages, you might benefit from asking a journalist (if you know them well) how you could have improved the release, but the general rule is that you put all of your efforts into writing a really good release which stands on its own.

Finally, never forget that a press release which is covered by the media has an opportunity to be seen by hundreds of thousands of people. PR people call this an OTS (opportunity to see). Not everyone will read every item in a newspaper, but everyone who buys it (or accesses it online) certainly has an opportunity to see it. What the press release is doing is putting the information in front of the person. The exposure is massive, even if it is a small amount of text. It is always worth the effort and it never ceases to amaze me that, months after a story is covered, you meet people who say, 'I was only reading about you recently.' That's what it's all about!

CASE STUDY – IRISH INDEPENDENT

This information is based on an interview with Kevin Doyle, former news editor of the Irish Independent *and currently their group political editor. He provides insight into what you should and shouldn't do if submitting a press release to the news desk of a media outlet.*

Things that you should ALWAYS do:

- Use bullet points.

- Include quotes from key people.

- Give information about imagery available.

- Focus on the top line – it is the key to success.

- Make it readable.

- Always provide a mobile number.

- Be available to take calls from journalists.

Things that you should NEVER do:

- Phone to ask, 'Did you get my email?'

- Phone with pointless information.

- Phone on the deadline.

- Look for advice on where you went wrong!

Kevin recommends that in general all companies issuing press releases to the news media should take the following steps:

1   Find out who is the person who covers your area of business or your kind of story.

2   Send a personalised email two to three days in advance of issuing information: 'Hello. Mind if I give you a quick call? I want to introduce myself and tell you what we are doing.' Journalists tend to reply to this kind of email, so it is always worth sending.

3   Have case studies ready of how the product impacts on real people. For example, for companies in the pharmaceutical area, if there is a new invention or product which helps control asthma, have a mother of three ready. Case studies are about real people – the child who spent all his time indoors is now able to play hopscotch. Have a different case study for each paper. If you have just one, perhaps you should offer it exclusively to one newspaper, the one which is read by most of your main audience.

When submitting a press release to a specific newspaper, one of the first things that you should do is watch what else is happening on the day. The news desk of the *Irish Independent* holds its first conference of the day at 11.30 a.m. This provides an outline of the key news stories for that day's paper. It is a map of what is happening. So issuing press releases early in the day is better. You should have your release in before the first morning news conference if possible. But before sending in the release, listen to the radio or turn on the early morning TV to find out what's making the news that day and, depending on the stories, perhaps hold on to the release for one more day.

For example, you might be issuing a release as a small pharmaceutical company, but if the health correspondents are flat out covering a major story they won't look at your release. And remember that you cannot reissue it. Once you have sent the release it is dead. If the paper didn't cover it on Monday, they won't appreciate you reissuing it on Tuesday – in fact, you'll probably just aggravate them!

Bear in mind that your release could have been good, but it was just unlucky. For example, if a pharma release lands on the news editor's desk on the same day that the government decides to abandon Universal Health Insurance, it will probably not be covered. A lot of space gets devoted to analysis and comment about major issues, but there is only so much that people will read around an issue. Having read extensively about, in this example, Universal Health Care, the news editor and reader might be in telepathic agreement that no more health-related stories would be relevant on the day.

Also remember that if the paper says that they want an exclusive, it means that they are definitely planning to use it – but if a big global story happens (like a terrorist attack in a major European city) your story may well fall by the wayside. After the day when they have said they will use it you are free to send it to other media. Nothing is 100 per cent – but a request for an exclusive certainly means that they will try to cover it.

Between 9 a.m. and 11 a.m. is the ideal time to send a press release (and you use the same time of day if issuing on Sunday for Monday's papers). Sunday is a quieter day in terms of hard news (no politics or courts), so it can be a very good day to issue soft news.

It can help to send a diary notice for an event or for research, i.e. advance notification that information of interest to them will be issued in a few days' time (always specify the exact day and outline the nature of the information). This allows the news desk to see if the story would fit beside another story that it is planning to run. Health and politics tend to be bunched together in a paper, so advance notice for these areas in particular is always good.

When choosing who to send the press release to, Kevin cautions against sending it to everyone. Although the news desk reads all press releases (from consultancies, small firms, everybody), he recommends that you develop a relationship with the journalist who covers your area of business. A PR consultancy may have a pre-existing relationship with a specific journalist or editor. If the journalist knows you or the PR company working for you, then the paper will know that you have form, i.e. your stuff stands up to scrutiny and the paper has published it in the past. Phone and ask the journalist if they have an interest in the story. You are far better to ring the journalist ten times than ring the news desk. The news desk doesn't have an interest in a specific area. Also, journalists are constantly looking for stories to feed to the news desk.

Developing this sort of relationship also means that if the journalist gets used to you as a source of good information, about travel for example, they might contact you when the CSO statistics come out and ask you for a quote.

Despite this, make sure you always send a press release to the news desk as well, even if you are sending it to a journalist in the paper. The news desk sees the bigger picture – there might be an environmental special in the paper the following day and your press release information might fit better there.

Don't, whatever you do, oversell a story. Journalists find it very annoying when they receive press releases that do this, and it happens a lot. News desks often pass a story to a journalist to cover, only for the journalist to realise that there isn't a story there. 'The first time there's ever been ...' catches the eye of the news desk, but when the journalist does a little research, they find that it's not the first time at all. This could discourage them from looking at future releases from your company.

Always remember, a press release must have value. If the information is always poor, the journalists will know that your releases are always rubbish and they will stop reading them. But if you issue once a month, or once a quarter, and there is always a nugget in there, your release will be read.

For the press release itself, Kevin says, the length depends on the subject matter. It should start with a short summary and bullet points, then lead into the body of the text. Bullet points give focus. After that, your release can be as long as you like, but no news editor ever reads the whole thing. As a rule, if the summary and bullets are interesting, the editor will assign the information to a reporter.

The rule that you should use short words and short sentences still applies. The best press releases turn up in the paper almost unedited. You should put the most important information at the top and go from there. The top line is key to your success. It is the most important line of the release, and the first paragraph is the most important piece of text. Spend most of your time on those areas. They are the difference between success and failure. Make the entire text as readable as possible. Try to make figures, statistics and costs as easy to understand as possible.

Think about the audience. A tabloid will have a different focus than a broadsheet. If you are looking at a change in minimum wages, for example, *The Sun* might applaud the move as brilliant, while the *Irish Independent* might cover business concerns about how this will affect Ireland's competitiveness. Write with different audiences in mind.

Celebrity helps. Of that there is no doubt. Even in quotes it is better to have a well-known name, but it depends on the scenario. If your company has commissioned the research and you are in control of all of the content, then you can make yourself the expert on that issue.

Be sure to include information on any imagery that is available. At the bottom of the release, always make a note that pictures of XYZ have been sent to the picture desk, or an agency will be filing pictures later in the day. Make sure that the photo captions include search words that relate to the story. Caption information should always be embedded in the photos (captions attached by email have a far lower chance of even making it into the system to be looked at).

Photo quality is hugely important. Kevin feels that companies often scrimp on photography. Photos must be high resolution if you are sending them to a newspaper. Anyone can snap a picture, but the photos you need have to be specific to media. A media photographer (either a press or a PR photographer) will know the kind of photos that newspapers are looking for. Get a professional photographer. Don't use a smartphone! (Obviously, the rules are different if you are issuing online or you are reporting on a very fast-breaking live story.)

Kevin stresses that you should be sure that the name and mobile number at the bottom of the release belongs to someone who has been briefed about the contents and that the person is ready to take calls for four to five hours immediately after the release has been issued. You will lose the space in the newspaper if you are 'just in a meeting right now' and cannot respond quickly. When the news editor checks on progress and is told that the journalist is waiting for someone to get back to them, the usual response is to select another story and run with it instead. The media works to tight deadlines.

When sending in a press release, put it in the body of the email, as attachments aren't read. They take time to open and the format might not be compatible with the system the journalist is using. A very large percentage of them, as a result, are never opened. Journalists skim read emails to see if anything is of interest. If your release is going to a dedicated press release email address (inews@independent.ie for the physical *Irish Independent*, digital@independent.ie for the online version and so on) you don't have to say press release in the subject line.

Once you have submitted your release, do not drive journalists or news desks crazy with phone calls. The most aggravating is 'Did you get my email?' to which a polite response is 'Did you get a bounced-back notice?' People are busy and really don't have time to take pointless calls. You can phone if there is a new development or an additional piece of information, which has just come to light, but not on the day of submission.

Kevin has strong words for new companies issuing releases for the first time who ring to find out why they have not been covered and how they could improve on what they sent. 'We're not consultants to tell you how to do your job,' he says. 'Get someone trained in how to do it. Why should we offer you advice on where you went wrong? Learn the tools of the trade,' he adds.

He finishes by stressing that there is no limit to the number of times, or press releases, that you can submit to a newspaper. Just because you weren't covered the first six times doesn't mean that they won't cover the next one.

2

THIRD-PARTY ENDORSEMENT

If you look at any of the big brands, you will see that they all use some form of third-party endorsement. The idea is almost as old as the hills. As early as 1952, movie star Elizabeth Taylor was advertising Lux soap. 'My skin is so much softer' the ad said. The ad wasn't selling Lux soap as such. It was selling the belief to women all over the world that if they used Lux soap they could be as beautiful as Elizabeth Taylor. Don't scoff. It's a powerful tool.

Look at the amount of money that former footballer David Beckham makes from endorsements. He endorses underwear, football boots, watches, shaving razors, whiskey, soft drinks, aftershave, technology, property ... even fish fingers! It's an amazing range of goods. Everyone wants a piece of Beckham's elusive 'star quality'. Sales rocket when his name is associated with a product – that's why companies are happy to pay him huge sums of money to endorse their products. I have heard it said that it wouldn't matter if Beckham was completely bald when he launched a new shampoo, it would still sell well because his name is attached.

Years ago brand names sometimes became confused with the actual product. Hoover was a brand name that people started to use as a descriptor of the function (I need to hoover). Nowadays, we all live branded lifestyles. Listen to how people speak. They describe items by brand. They have a Nokia or a Galaxy (not a phone), they wear Jimmy Choo's (not high heels), they wear Nike, Reebok or Adidas (not runners). Brands reinforce our self-image and tell the world something about who we are. That is how they are promoted. So who you are is reflected in the people who endorse the brand that you use.

Chanel No. 5 used to be a perfume that was targeted at an older generation, until Nicole Kidman became associated with it in the famous 'Paris' advertisement. Suddenly the perfume was cool because she was. In fact, Chanel went on to use a number of high-profile women. They even used Brad Pitt to endorse their No. 5 perfume. He was the first man ever to do so!

Look at the advertising for L'Oréal. It's superb. It connects with the psyche. It appeals to people to be a little self-indulgent. It encourages them to pamper themselves a little. Buy our shampoo 'because you're worth it'.

Endorsement is not all about product though. It is also about organisations. The United Nations has Carl Lewis (athletics) and Ronaldo (footballer) among its goodwill ambassadors. UNICEF's most famous ambassador is probably Mia Farrow, but the Irish are well represented by Liam Neeson, Rory McIlroy, Pierce Brosnan, Cathy Kelly and Stephen Rea. All of these people bring their values, their life experience and their sincerity to the job. Because of their fame, they attract media attention, so working for the UN or UNICEF on a visit ensures that the world's media will be focused on that area. In this case the endorsement is for a very different reason. It is not that people subscribe to either organisation because of the fame of their ambassadors. Rather, the ambassadors bring an added credibility and clout to the organisations by allowing their names to be used in support of what they are doing.

In Ireland, the most famous endorser is the president. For example, he is president of the Irish Red Cross. His patronage ensures that anyone looking at the organisation from the outside in will be quite sure that this is a well-conducted organisation which does good work and is endorsed by the person of highest standing in the country.

Very often, when charities are seeking to raise money for good causes, they ask famous people to attend functions, speak and be photographed at them. To be fair to Irish celebrities, they are absolutely wonderful at giving their time, free, to charities which they support or endorse. Although it was later mired in controversy, I have no doubt that people were encouraged to support the

Central Remedial Clinic's Santa Bear promotion because of the support of Ronan Collins, who is a greatly loved and respected RTÉ presenter.

Politicians also lend their endorsement to events by attending. They will always attend functions free of charge – and this is only right and proper. When you invite a local politician or the lord mayor, a minister or the taoiseach to attend a function, you are inviting a public representative. You invite the 'office' as much as you invite the individual. (From a business perspective, it does not matter, for example, what political party the person is from. What matters is the public office they hold.) Politicians need to be booked well in advance – they are in huge demand – and ministers will set criteria for functions that they attend. Often a minister will attend a small function if it is in their constituency, but might insist on a minimum of 500 people attending, or 50 jobs being created, or a €5m investment before their civil servants will consider making them available outside of the constituency. This ensures that the minister is not run ragged!

Herein lies a very important point: celebrities attract attention. Ordinary people want to meet them, shake their hands, say that they chatted with them and have their photos taken with them. The celebrity also brings a certain amount of media attention with them. However, celebrities can also earn money from appearances. It is fairly true to say that if you are on television in Ireland, most of the country is curious to see what you really look like in the flesh. Celebrities charge money to corporate bodies to attend their events, endorse their products, chair their conferences, speak at their seminars, introduce their award ceremonies and be photographed with the company's key people. This is all perfectly valid.

From your point of view as a business, you want a little of that association as well. But it can be very expensive. Begin by looking at who you know (or who you can get an introduction to), who might have an interest in what you are doing. Once you start looking, it is amazing the access you can get because of someone living next door, or having a child on the same school rugby team, for example. It is possible that someone in the company is the brother or sister of a county hurler or footballer. They might oblige just because they are asked. Does anyone belong to a business group that has a famous member or two? Would they endorse your product? Can you connect with someone via LinkedIn and ask for their endorsement?

The difficulty with using people you have access to is that they may not be the people who are actually respected by your target audience (we're back to that old chestnut of finding out what your audience is interested in). You might be better to wait until you can afford the right person rather than using someone who is available to you.

In today's world there are also the celebrities who only exist on YouTube. They have no media presence beyond that platform, but have thousands of followers and make a good living from doing appearances. They might well be the celebrities who are of most interest to your audience – especially if your business operates in an online environment.

When looking for a third-party endorser your first job, as always, is to research your target market. Who are you selling to and what are their interests? Some research in the early stages will prevent you from making costly mistakes. The Irish Academy of Public Relations organised a function some years ago where the MD of the company asked if we would use a certain celebrity as an endorser. We were very conscious that the actress hadn't been in huge demand, publicly, for a number of years. We suggested that she was an inappropriate choice and, to add weight to the argument, asked for a profile of the company's target audience. We then did some unscientific research on the main street of the local town, asking people to tell us something about several actors of that era. Most people in the target age group (mid-twenties to mid-thirties) had no idea who we were asking about (the fifty-plus age group knew the actress). The MD agreed to use a different celebrity.

Be careful of choosing just one endorser. If something

goes wrong – if they are convicted of drink driving or found in possession of drugs – it will reflect on your company. Better to choose several endorsers or a team if possible.

Why do you need celebrity endorsement? Because people like to check you out and they like to know that other people think your product is good. To a certain extent this need can be answered by the testimonials on your website. You should always, by the way, show that these are real people. At a minimum, use their full names and possibly their location in the world. Otherwise, there is a good chance that people will think that your testimonials are made up. If possible also use photographs so that people visiting the site can see that others like and believe in your product.

Celebrity endorsers perform a different function, however. People are happy to know that people just like themselves use your product or buy from your company or support your charity, but it is nice to know that people in the public eye, people that they and their friends admire, also use your product or buy from your company. Now your potential clients are sure that they are in good hands. They not only mix in a circle that buys from you, but they aspire to mix in another circle that thinks you are great. Psychologically it's a strong selling tool and a great way of creating subliminal images in the minds of your clients.

Just before I close, let me focus for a moment on what happens if you choose the wrong endorser. The wrong choice will send the wrong message and, instead of bringing people to your business, it will drive them away. For example, let's assume that you are producing a range of clothing for female city-slickers whose interests are movies, meals, fashion and clubbing. You get access to the winning captain of an all-Ireland sports team and decide to use her as your endorser. Your target audience has nothing in common with her and may not know her. They will stop buying your clothes because they are 'obviously' not for them, they are for sporty people. Similarly if your product is targeting the over-fifties and you use an up-and-coming twenty-year-old model, your target audience will leave believing that they have misidentified the product.

So, you can drive business away with the wrong endorser. Choose carefully.

CASE STUDY – NEWBRIDGE SILVERWARE

This case study is based on an interview with Marie Brennan, Communications Manager with Newbridge Silverware.

Newbridge Silverware has been around since 1934. Although it started life as a government initiative, it became a private company when it was bought by Dominic Doyle in the 1970s. The company was going through a tough time because of the economic downturn, and Doyle reviewed their product range and adapted it to suit the styles of the time.

The first jewellery line was made from the off-cuts of their silver-plated cutlery. When the cutlery shapes had been cut, the remaining silver plate had really ornate shapes left in it and the idea of polishing these and making pieces of jewellery from them was raised. The jewellery range began production in the 1990s. Needless to say, the entire process is very different now.

Newbridge constantly monitors trends and realised that all of the luxury brands around the world (across all industries) were advertising using famous faces. It decided to adopt this strategy, but in a different way. The idea of using third-party endorsers – or 'Newbridge Ambassadors' as they are known – was born.

Newbridge began to advertise using famous Irish faces to promote Irish products. Andrea Roche was the first 'Newbridge Ambassador'. At the time she was a well-known model in Ireland and the reigning Miss Ireland. She was someone that people admired and aspired to be.

Anne Doyle was another face associated with Newbridge jewellery from the early days. That association came about in a different way. It was Anne who approached William Doyle (who had taken over the running of the business from his father, Dominic) and asked if she could get on board. She had heard that Newbridge had created a jewellery line and said she'd support it and wear it on *RTÉ News*. Anne really was the face of the news in Ireland at the time and, although she has since left RTÉ, she is still very popular with the public at large. In fact, hers is the voice that is still used on the Newbridge telephone system to this day.

The endorsers haven't all been women. Three men, all with rugby associations, have been ambassadors for Newbridge. Keith Wood, the Munster rugby player, was the first of these. He promoted a cookware line. He was followed by Ronan O'Gara, who promoted goods across the entire range. Currently Newbridge is working with Rob Kearney, who is promoting the 'Guinness by Newbridge' homeware line. It's a partnership with Guinness and the first time that Newbridge has jointly worked with another company to create something like this. The range includes casserole dishes and textiles. It is a neutral brand line that works well for both genders. There is also a well-known photo of Kearney wearing Newbridge cufflinks and a watch.

In 2006 Newbridge created the Museum of Style Icons. It is funny how these things come about. William Doyle was on holiday when he read in *Hello* magazine that the iconic black Givenchy dress worn by Audrey Hepburn in *Breakfast at Tiffany's* would be auctioned at Christie's in London. He decided to buy it. As it transpired, William was the under bidder – Givenchy bought the dress for £650,000. They were never going to let someone else have it.

The next dress up for auction was a dress that Hepburn wore in *Charade*, so William bought that one instead. Buying celebrity dresses has become a huge industry now, but it wasn't when William started. The Newbridge museum now has the largest collection of Audrey Hepburn dresses worldwide!

It has since added collections from three other style icons to its catalogue – Grace Kelly, Greta Garbo and Maureen O'Hara. The museum worked directly with O'Hara when she was alive, and also works with the Grace Kelly and Greta Garbo foundations.

Back to the 'Newbridge Ambassadors'. In the early 2000s the company worked with Linda Gray and Larry Hagman from the television series *Dallas*. Then, in 2006, Yasmin le Bon began working with the brand. She was an international superstar and Newbridge's first proper ambassador. Her contract was for a one-year period. She was hired to endorse its products, and the contract included photography for that season's brochure, which was also used for public relations, advertising and point of sale. (This was the era before the growth of the web and social media!)

Yasmin le Bon came to Ireland (she is UK-based) and, as the face of Newbridge, judged the 'Best Dressed Lady' competition at the Punchestown races which Newbridge sponsored. (Linda Gray and Larry Hagman had done it previously.) She attended the Showcase exhibition, an annual exhibition for craftspeople that attracts an international audience of buyers, and met the company's retailers. She also visited the Newbridge visitor centre for a day.

It was not an exclusive deal. The contract did not stipulate that she could wear only Newbridge silver. An endorsement has to be real. If it is not, Newbridge believes, it will look contrived. It wants its ambassadors to have their own style, one which includes Newbridge jewellery.

The contract, then and since, has always included a clause that either party can break the contract for extenuating circumstances. It is a get-out clause, which provides comfort on both sides. If either Newbridge or the ambassador does something which is completely against brand guidelines, then either side can end the arrangement.

Yasmin le Bon was followed by Sophie Dahl, another international face from the world of modelling, who was again contracted for one year. Then the recession hit. Like every brand in Ireland, Newbridge was trying to minimise costs and didn't hire a new celebrity ambassador after Dahl's contract came to an end. The company had to adapt and, instead, began to really promote its style icons. Over a three-year period, from 2007 to 2009, it bought lots of clothes belonging to the three icons and also worked closely with O'Hara and the Garbo and Kelly foundations to create three jewellery collections.

The reinvention of the 'Newbridge Ambassador' happened in 2013, when Amy Huberman signed a two-year contract. Once again, the contract did not stipulate that she must wear only Newbridge jewellery. She was the face of the brand, however, and Newbridge did its first TV commercial with her. Two advertisements were created, one for homeware and the other for jewellery. A long and short version of each was made, which were used on TV and in cinemas.

When Amy started working with Newbridge, it was because the company wanted to give the brand another push. Many international competitors had come into Ireland in the intervening years. Amy has a UK fan base, but she was primarily chosen for her appeal to Irish people. Moreover, as a notable Irish celebrity, she was only going to choose a few brands to work with so that she could protect her own brand.

She proved to be a popular choice with consumers, retailers and the media. The entire product offering and brand had been re-invented. For the advertising campaign, Newbridge worked closely with her individual style and picked out pieces that she would actually wear. She was kept in the loop throughout the decision-making process and the partnership worked really well. This was the first real through-the-line relationship for Newbridge. It was all about re-inventing the brand and evolving with changing consumer tastes. Newbridge honestly believes that a brand cannot be stagnant. If it is, it will become irrelevant.

One of the big advantages of having Amy Huberman as its ambassador was that she tweets and has a lot of Twitter followers. Although this was not part of her contract, she chose to tweet about Newbridge jewellery, which boosted sales. Newbridge believes that this was a direct result of the strong relationship it had with her as an ambassador. In fact, Amy announced that she was expecting her second baby in a tweet which read:

> Thanks for all the lovely messages! #ootd coat by Cos, necklace by @newbridgesilver, bump by @BrianODriscoll x

The photo showed Amy in a really long necklace by Newbridge. The power of that one tweet was insane. The necklace sold out and when Newbridge did another large run, that sold out too!

If the ambassador doesn't believe in the association, then it's not going to work. It must be a credible and real partnership. Both sides have to buy into it for it to work.

Naomi Campbell is the current ambassador and is signed for a two-year period. The prime target audience is females who are thirty-five and older. As part of the photo-shoot to announce their new ambassador, Naomi was pictured wearing a silver bodice (previously worn by Yasmin le Bon). She is forty-four years old and looked amazing. Newbridge is currently expanding in the UK and USA and Naomi is helping them, particularly in the UK. The company is not doing TV advertising at present and is reviewing its strategy due to the huge changes in advertising over the last ten years. Instead it is working on a new advertising plan.

Newbridge retains strong relationships with its ambassadors. Even when they are no longer officially connected to the company they remain 'Friends of Newbridge'.

HOW TO GET STARTED

Newbridge's philosophy is that working with brand ambassadors or third-party endorsers is not dependent on the size of the company. The most important thing is that a company gets the right 'fit'. If an SME is choosing an endorser, then an up-and-coming person is going to be more cost-effective than an established name. Take a chance and it could work out very well. It's all about both parties having the right attitude.

It's also important that the company pitches themselves correctly to the celebrity. How you do it is key. Make a good pitch! Impress the person. Get them to buy into your vision.

The contract is vital for both parties. Get good legal advice but don't forget to involve non-legal people as well. Experts in marketing and PR will identify different angles that might be included in the contract, which will help you to cross off a lot of business objectives.

The budget is really determined by the nature and size of the business. However, Newbridge says that it is nearly the last thing that you should discuss. All of the other factors come first.

You can approach your endorser/ambassador directly or through an agent, but Newbridge is adamant that no PR company should start the relationship. The discussions and contacts should be directly between the business and the celebrity, with very few people in between. (The more people involved, the more complicated things become, and this moves the focus away from the core relationship between brand and endorser.)

Newbridge also feels strongly that time spent nurturing a good relationship with an ambassador will yield additional dividends for the business. Think about all of the business objectives that the ambassador can help you achieve – not just the column inches – and don't forget that they can also be used at a private event for your best customers.

3

PRESS RECEPTIONS

A press reception can attract a lot of media attention and create some very powerful visuals around your business. It is a great way of bringing an audience of people together and getting the press to witness and report on something happening. We live in a mediated age, where people are overtly influenced by what they read, see and hear. Real life is in some ways secondary to the 'lived' experience that people have through their online presence and great store can be attached to the company that you, corporately, keep. Good publicity from a press reception, both online and in traditional media, can therefore be of great benefit to your business.

For many years, I served on the board of the Corporate Social Responsibility (CSR) Committee of Chambers Ireland. I was invited onto the committee because my business, the Irish Academy of Public Relations, won a CSR Award for our work in raising funds for charitable causes.

Each year, Chambers Ireland holds a press reception to announce the opening of the CSR Awards. The event is held mid-morning in a city centre hotel and I'm guessing that approximately 300–400 business people attend. I have no idea why it is so popular but it always attracts a great crowd. There are at least two speeches – one from the organisers explaining how the event will be run for the coming year, and one from the sponsors talking about what they will be looking for. A guest speaker is also usually invited, to discuss or highlight an issue of concern (suicide, for example, was a theme in a previous year). The media are invited to attend, and are given press releases and opportunities to interview the main participants and photograph all of those attending the event. There is always a great buzz about the place, and the Chambers of Commerce get great photos to use for their various magazines, websites, Facebook pages and other social media platforms. The media, in turn, have an opportunity to find out what trends, if any, are expected to surface in the coming year and to learn a little more about the value of CSR in Ireland. From the organiser's point of view, the benefit of the press reception is that it gives the media access to key players and the chance to photograph leaders of the business community lending their support to a great initiative.

Press receptions can also be used to announce events, such as the sponsorship of Ladies' Day at a local horse-racing meet. For this kind of occasion, the organisers would go to a lot of trouble to ensure that jockeys, trainers and owners were present so that the media would have an opportunity to photograph them away from their usual environment. These events are usually glamorous affairs with models attending; the previous winner of Ladies' Day would also often appear and possibly some celebrities associated with the area. The models are probably being paid to attend, so the event is expensive to run, but the benefit is that the ordinary punter reading the papers doesn't know this and assumes that horse racing has a certain cachet about it which attracts this type of person. In addition, the women who are being targeted for the best-dressed lady event are influenced by the models attending. Many people will see the coverage on media and social media. The press reception might be quite a short affair but the publicity it generates can be used for national, local, magazine, blogger and social media coverage.

Not all press receptions need celebrities to be brought in specially. The Irish Academy of Public Relations handled a press reception for a team of athletes returning from the United States Cerebral Palsy Athletic Association National Games, an international games meet. The purpose of the reception was to give the media an opportunity to attend, hear some speeches from the organisers and sponsors, meet the athletes and provide them with the chance to photograph the winners wearing their medals. In this case, we did not need to bring any other celebrities to the event, as the athletes themselves were the celebrities on that occasion.

A press reception might also be held to announce the sponsors for an event, such as a local summer festival. In that case, if your company is one of the sponsors attending, rather than the organiser, you need to be sure that you get the maximum benefit from being there. For example, if the organisers are bringing a guest celebrity to open the event – let's say it's former Miss World Rosanna Davison – then you need to be sure that they arrange for you to be photographed with her. The photographs may or may not be picked up by the media – they will certainly use her photograph but it might not be with you – but the organisers will use the photos for local media, on their own website and Facebook pages, and you can certainly tweet about them and post and link to other sites. The photos can also be used in a company brochure later, when you are writing about your connections with the local community.

Press receptions are not always evening events, although that twilight zone of 6–8 p.m. is very popular. Dublin City fm regularly holds press receptions at that time to announce the new schedule for the station. It is the radio station for Dublin city, broadcasts for nineteen hours every day and has a schedule of programmes to rival RTÉ in terms of number and breadth. The station broadcasts programmes for the wider Dublin community of Russians, Africans, Indians, Polish and Koreans. There are shows about books, sport, media, current affairs, Bollywood, genre music – even Little Steven from Bruce Springsteen's E-Street Band broadcasts on the station. The station's press receptions give the media an opportunity to find out what is new or changing in Dublin city and how that is being reflected in the new schedule. Because the station also broadcasts a weekly interview with the lord mayor, and works closely with Dublin City Council for the broadcast of *LiveDrive* – the station's motoring programme – the lord mayor has been a keynote speaker at their press receptions in the past.

The point of a press reception is to get media journalists and photographers to attend, photograph and report on the event. It is important, therefore, that you actually have something to say and people to photograph. If you promise the media that celebrities will attend, then you must produce them. If you say that people 'might' be there that also means that they 'might not', so media representatives are much less likely to attend. If you say that people 'will' be there, it probably means that there is a commercial arrangement in place. It also means that your celebrities are willing to be photographed. If people attend in a private capacity, even if they are public faces, they are perfectly entitled to refuse to be photographed.

So what do you need if you are hosting a press reception? Well, in the first instance, you need a topic which will interest the local and/or national media enough for them to want to attend. The media is inundated with invitations to functions, so you will have to work hard to make sure that your event has all the winning elements.

Once you have the topic, you need to decide where the event will be held. You might choose a local hotel, or perhaps there is an opportunity to have the reception on a houseboat (if you're near a canal) or on a special bus travelling around the city, or in your corporate headquarters. Be careful about using your HQ though. It needs to attract the media. I have attended press receptions in the Google building in Dublin and it is amazing. It is nothing like a normal corporate office – and that, of course, is part of the attraction. Media and guests alike love it. You should avoid holding press receptions at your HQ if it fails to stand out.

When you know where you are holding the event, you need to decide what you will serve at the reception. Mid-morning events usually have tea/coffee and biscuits or scones; lunchtime receptions can be as simple as soup and sandwiches; evening receptions can be wine and canapés. Food and drink can make a real difference, so it is worth putting a little thought into these things. You should always have non-alcoholic beverages available whether you are offering alcohol or not. If your press reception is about healthy living, maybe you could include a note with your media invitation that the reception will serve frozen watermelon slushies, power smoothies and combination fruit juices. Or if your reception is to launch a new travel brochure, you might serve samples of food from the areas included, for example Airag (made from mare's milk) from Mongolia, or luscious apple strudel from Austria. To launch a winter wonderland outdoor market, your press reception might serve hot chocolate and toasted marshmallows. You need to put some effort into creating a reception that your guests, and particularly the media, will want to attend.

Then you need to tempt them with details of who will attend. You might have Santa and his helpers attending the launch of the Christmas fair. You might also notify the media that the helpers are all from a well-known model agency, so that they know they can be sure of photogenic subjects and great poses! Your invitation to a press reception to launch a new movie app might state that James Bond, the Terminator, Marilyn Monroe and Lara Croft will be among the 'stars' attending. Again the media knows that they are guaranteed people to photograph.

A few years ago the Irish Academy of Public Relations held a press reception on a fishing trawler. It was to let the media know that the proceeds of the gala opening of a particular film in Dublin were going to a charity we represented. Much of the action in the movie took place on a fishing trawler, so we decided to invite the media to take a short trip up the River Liffey and into Dublin Bay while we told them all about the movie and the beneficiaries of the opening night. It was something a bit different and the media responded really well.

When my book, *Capital Women of Influence*, was launched a few years ago, I held a press reception in the Irish Writers' Centre on Parnell Square. There were two key media attractions on the night. The first was Senator David Norris, who launched the book and was wonderfully witty, outrageously 'Dub', scathingly perceptive and utterly adored by everyone present. The entire audience was 'putty in his paws'. He is a man guaranteed to provide quotable sound bites for the media. The other attraction was the women who were profiled in the book. Caroline Downey, Veronica Dunne, Pauline Bewick, Evelyn Byrne, Gina Quinn and Betty Ashe were all present and were a huge media attraction.

For any event like this you should always book your own photographer so that you have photos to use afterwards – or to send to any media who could not attend. Use a professional photographer. You also need to be clear about a start and finish time, and, if possible, give details of a running order. Let the media know who will speak, in what order and for how long. Press receptions generally last from an hour up to ninety minutes.

Finally, it is important that you never confuse a press reception with a press conference. A reception is a light and fluffy event to generate publicity. A conference is generally a response to a crisis, where, often, a pre-prepared statement is made and the media are then given the chance to question key participants to gain further information about the situation.

CASE STUDY – THE MODERN JOURNALIST

This case study is based on an interview with John Meagher, features writer, broadcaster and music critic.

John Meagher is quite typical of the modern journalist. He left the Independent group in summer 2015 to work for himself. He now freelances for the *Irish Independent*, the *Irish Examiner* magazine, *Arena* on RTÉ radio and also works as a copywriter for *Discover Ireland*. He works about a sixty-hour week. So, unless he is aware of the value to him of going to a reception, he won't go. He simply doesn't have the time to spare!

One of the press receptions that he does always attend is the one held for Electric Picnic. The first Electric Picnic event wasn't that good he says, but he persevered and it was better the second year and has been great every year since. The attraction of attending for John is a mixture of things:

– He likes the people involved. They are good at what they do. They choose interesting venues, which are accessible but different. (In 2015 it was the Chocolate Factory off Parnell Street in Dublin.)

– It's always a good gig. It's cool. They always have a good band playing. It is an 'event' worth attending.

– He can network. He knows that he is going to meet every

other music critic in Dublin at the event because, by now, it is well established on the journalists' calendar. He will also meet all of the PR people who are relevant to the music industry.

— It creates opportunities. He might get an interview with a band further down the road.

All of these things benefit him as a journalist, so he knows he won't be wasting his time attending.

Untailored media lists are a particular bugbear of his. People pepper out invitations to every journalist they can think of, whether it is relevant to them or not. It is important for any press reception that you invite journalists who know they will feel it has been worth their while turning up and won't come away feeling disappointed. John is adamant that when companies are inviting journalists to attend press receptions, they need to be very targeted in their approach. He thinks that often there is a focus on quantity rather than quality, but it is far better to invite the few who are relevant, rather than the multitude. Companies will often invite 500 journalists to a reception, when only twenty of them might actually be interested in its subject.

Personally, John gets about ten invitations to press receptions every week, some of which are not related to his area of expertise. He has even received invitations to the launch of a new couture fashion range! He believes that companies should carefully select the journalists who might be interested and be able to deliver some coverage for them. It is also vital that they make contact with the journalist in advance and explain why this reception is suitable for them and their paper. It is very naive to think that journalists have such poor social lives that they are just waiting for an invitation to go somewhere!

Moreover, John believes that a lot of press receptions these days are actually aimed at bloggers rather than print journalists. Bloggers have a huge reach through social media, but they perform a different function. In fact, companies sometimes confuse the roles of blogger and journalists. We all hate for our time to be wasted, so it is important the companies do their homework and figure out who are the most relevant people to invite to their reception.

Many launches are also badly timed and are often scheduled for times which clash directly with newspaper deadlines. John thinks that some companies can be horribly presumptuous in assuming that journalists have any amount of time to turn up and can do so at the drop of a hat. Not so, he says. If the companies want specific people to be present, then they need to take the time to find out when will suit those they particularly want to attend their events.

For John, the end of the week is his busiest time. Wednesday to Friday is manic. Early in the week is best if you are trying to attract him to attend a function. He has been invited to functions at 6 p.m. on a Wednesday evening. Even if it was an amazing function, he says, he could not go because the review section of the paper goes to bed on Thursday at lunch-hour and he would usually be filing copy until 10 p.m. on Wednesday evening. He would not willingly lengthen his already long day!

An increasing trend in modern press receptions is to provide goody bags to attendees at the end of an event. As a general rule, there is no harm in that. John accepts that if you are the maker of soap for example, you might well want to give a sample of your product to people leaving your event. However, he dislikes the new trend of putting information about the goody bags and their contents onto the press invitations. He believes that this indicates that the person organising the event is looking for publicity based on a 'thank you' for the goody bag, when they should be concentrating on creating a good story for the journalists to cover.

He also deplores the fact that junior members of staff, interns and job-bridge people are asked to phone journalists to check if they are attending functions. The problem with these people is that they do not have a background in media and have not been properly briefed. Very often, they don't even have a clear notion of the paper he is working for. He has been asked, for example, about who should be phoned to get coverage in *The Ticket* (an *Irish Times* publication) or what the deadline is for the culture section of *The Sunday Times*. Neither of these papers has any connection with the Independent group for which he writes. Such a lack of basic information would not encourage him to attend future events run by those companies.

Location is another issue. He is constantly surprised by the fact that, although he is Dublin-based, he gets invitations to events down the country the next day. It simply beggars belief that companies would think that he is available to attend on such short notice, or that he would be interested in taking a train/driving to the event and possibly overnighting in a hotel, to cover it. The time and expense involved make this utterly unfeasible.

If a company is looking for national coverage for an event and they are trying to attract a journalist who is not local to cover it, he believes the press reception may not be the right approach. Instead, people need to be clever – they need to take a smarter approach and tailor the event.

He cites an event in Belfast as a personal example that impressed him greatly. Initially he received a phone call from the PR person asking if he was interested in the music scene in Belfast. As it happened, he was. The PR person then offered to bring him to Belfast, in conjunction with Tourism Northern Ireland, and put him up for a night. During his time in the city, they would bring him to view venues which were alive with music and musicians. One venue even had an exhibition running. It was a very specific opportunity for him and for Belfast. The focus was entirely on the music scene in Belfast and how vibrant it was. He learned a lot, enjoyed his stay, and wrote a 1,000-word piece about it for the *Irish Independent*. It is a clever example of the tourist board targeting a journalist in the largest-read national daily paper in Ireland and creating an event (tour and overnight) for him to attend, which generated good publicity for them. This was far better than simply inviting him to a press reception about the Belfast music scene, which he probably wouldn't have gone to.

John gives another example of specific targeting which resulted in good publicity (which, after all, is the object of the exercise). When the Point Depot was redeveloped, and was re-opening as the O2 arena, he got a call inviting him to take a pre-launch tour. The offer was made to ten journalists. They were brought in a week before the venue opened. Each was told that they could have as little or as much time as they wanted in the venue (there was great respect for how busy journalists actually are). They were asked if there were any specific areas they wanted to know more about, for example, the development of the venue, or the future promotion plans. They were given access to all areas and told that the tour of the venue would be targeted to their needs. Whatever they needed, they got. This was a very commercial brand seeking publicity from a national newspaper. Their offer was very curated and very specific – and it worked. As a result, John wrote a major piece for *Day and Night* magazine.

In addition to this, there was a champagne launch for the glitterati, more like a normal press reception. It too was well covered by media, particularly what John calls 'next-day journalists', who needed copy for their papers for the following day. John, however, did not attend. He already had his story written. From the venue's point of view, they had his story in train and were now seeking a different kind of publicity from the champagne reception – by being smart, they got two bites of the publicity apple.

4

PHOTO CALLS

We live in a very visual era. Videos are a great way to promote your business online. People love looking at infographics on social media. Photographs are consumed in traditional and new media. Pictures make it easy to see, absorb, understand – and move on! We are a time poor society, which makes photographs more important than they have ever been.

Photos can be a visual record of what happened – the new factory opening, the launch of an extension to the building, the formation of a new political party, the signing of a joint-venture agreement, the announcement of new jobs created, the visit of an American partner company, etc. This type of photo – historical – is incredibly valuable for websites, annual reports, newsletters, ezines, social media, even for the walls of the office.

Media photos, on the other hand, are a different creature altogether. When you organise a photo call for media you are not asking them to historically record something. You are, instead, inviting them to something you have visually created which tells a story that you believe their readers would be interested in. So you need to create a visual that the public will want to look at.

Some things are easy to create visuals for. If you are a waste disposal company and you are expanding into southern Ireland, for example, you can create a photo of bags of rubbish, your bin truck, binmen (or are they bin persons – I've never seen a woman in this role!), seagulls – real or fake – and really make an interesting photo with those ingredients. If you are opening a new state-of-the-art laundry facility, it is slightly easier. In this case, you have modern equipment.

The first thing you need to do is create an interesting photo. So what makes photos interesting? Think of the shots that you look at yourself – you are drawn to them for a reason. It might be that someone was doing something unusual (a waiter walking out of the sea with a silver salver in his hand), or it might be that the person in it is a well-known celebrity (Marty Whelan wearing big yellow wellies). It could be that a politician (Minister Bruton meeting people in white coats and plastic hats) or a well-known model is involved (Nadia Forde doing something for road safety). It might be an older, time-worn face, a young farmer climbing into a vintage tractor, or a group of people on the top of a small building looking up at Croke Park Stadium. What mostly catches our eye is people. We are curious about people, we are drawn to their faces and we want to identify what they are doing.

What they are doing must be appropriate and relevant to the story. It needs to promote your business or your product. It must make sense and allow the reader to make a connection without you blatantly advertising something. For instance, the Irish Academy of Public Relations has organised photo calls where a minister and the CEO both wore hard-hats at a sod-turning ceremony (the picture is obviously about building). We had children in a home kitchen with a cook (all wearing aprons and hats) photographed to promote a new option for entertaining children at parties. We had transition-year students dressed in wigs and gowns photographed because they won an environmental prize for putting the world on trial! We had someone climbing a ladder photographed to suggest that they are achieving success. We had a minister photographed with young models wearing hats created by an over-fifties entrepreneur to promote older people entering the world of business. We had two women photographed holding a long scroll listing the twenty-seven pieces of HR legislation that apply to SMEs to signify their creation of a new business dealing with HR issues. And we organised a photo call from a hotel balcony overlooking the Aviva stadium to announce details of a conference to be held there.

Sometimes it is difficult to get props that tell a story, so you need to use people in unusual locations. You might organise a photo call on the roof of a building which has great views of the city. You might have pictures taken from the top of the stairs looking down into the stairwell and have your people looking up at the photographer. You might put people on the curve of an old staircase so that they appear in a shot without standing in a line. You can photograph people walking outdoors, sitting over a cup of tea chatting, in silhouette at a Georgian window frame, on a high Nelly bicycle. It is the location, in these instances, that make the photograph visually interesting.

You may also need to create props for your photos. If you are moving office, maybe you should have a giant key created so that the directors can climb the steps outside the new building with a key in their hands (you don't need to see the door or the building!). For one photo call we created a time capsule which was stocked with items representing that particular decade – the story was about the depletion of our natural resources. For another, about the launch of a new telephone service, we had an old-fashioned telephone made as a prop. We have also had tin badges specially designed and made so that group photos can be subtly branded.

You don't need to create all of your props – sometimes they occur naturally in the environment. For example, we've done a photo call in Dublin Zoo with the lemurs on children's shoulders! We've photographed guide dogs (active and passive) as part of a story about enabling blind people. We've photographed a chef holding a large piece of meat on a wooden slab with a cleaver. We've had photographs taken in a five star hotel, with waiting staff in the background. We've photographed children on a farm – in the milking parlour, feeding lambs, riding Connemara ponies.

A word of warning – be careful when arranging outdoor photo calls. This is Ireland, so you will always need an indoor alternative. Even if it is mid-summer, be prepared to shoot indoors if necessary.

If you are working with models you will book them through a model agency. The agency will tell you the fee, collect the instructions about what exactly you want (how the model should be dressed, for example), the purpose of the photos (for media distribution), the length of time that you need the model and whether or not the work is just photography or if you also require them to mix and mingle with your guests. Models are not cheap, but the fees are not extortionate either! You get what you pay for, so if you use an 'up and coming' model it might be perfect for a young fashion-savvy audience, but they might be unknown to an older audience who might have instantly recognised a more established and familiar face.

If you are working with celebrities, you have to book

them through their agent. They are expensive and can often have additional demands. In one instance, when we were interested in using a celebrity couple from England, they quoted us a fee (five figures for forty minutes) and also wanted first-class flights from the UK, airport collection by limo, transport by limo to the south of Ireland (where the function was to be held) and the same for the return journey. It added 50 per cent to the fee quoted.

Celebrities can also be just plain difficult. I spoke with a colleague recently who was working with a male celebrity who I would have regarded as a 'B' lister. He was booked for a video shoot which began at 7.30 a.m. In addition to the fee, he insisted on being collected from his hotel by limo, he required breakfast on arrival at the venue at 6.30 a.m. and he wanted his personal hairdresser on site for 7 a.m. During the shoot, which was outdoors in winter, there was a coffee break. He asked for hot cocoa. None was available. He was offered tea/coffee/soup instead. None of this was acceptable. A member of staff had to drive for about forty minutes to find a shop which sold cocoa to bring it back on site and make it for him. Such stories are not unusual, so check all of the details in advance. In defence of celebrities, however, I should add that he was working with a female celebrity who arrived thirty minutes before the shoot, dressed and ready for hair and make-up. No fuss. No drama. Just business.

Celebrities make their money from these appearances and you should brief them well in advance so that they know exactly what is required. Most will take the brief, absorb it, make it their own and do a wonderfully professional job for you. Knowing a little about the celebrity in advance will also help. Some are naturally good with children or older people – others are not. It will make a difference to your photos.

Politicians will also attend and participate in photo calls for you. Do not underestimate the power of having a politician present at a business function. In Ireland, politicians are very accessible so we are inclined to underestimate their power to impress. For a corporate report, and particularly for any foreign business visits, the presence of the member of parliament, senator, minister or taoiseach in your photographs really carries weight.

The difficulty with politicians is that they will step into all photos and may be over-used (the media might be tired of using the same face day in, day out, week in, week out). The same is also true of celebrities. You want someone who is popular but not over-used.

Choose the time of day carefully. You want to create your photograph during natural daylight, if possible, and at a time when media can respond, attend and potentially use your photo. Generally photo calls should not happen before 10 a.m. in the morning or after 3.30 p.m. in the afternoon. Traditional media is still based in the city centre in Dublin, so try to choose a location which is convenient for them. There are fine hotels and buildings which can be used in the city centre, and outdoor locations like St Stephen's Green can create the illusion of 'the country'. Be careful to secure the relevant permissions for photographing in public places. Check with hotel and shopping centre owner/managers, city council park departments or railway station directors. If you don't own the location in which you are photographing it's always best to ask permission in advance.

They say that you should never work with children and animals. They are, certainly, unpredictable. They seldom do exactly what they are told. They can be unruly, plain bold and difficult. But you can also get the most amazing photos. If you are photographing children, you will need the written consent of a parent or guardian for every child in the photo. If you are photographing a football match, or re-constructing a scene from a play, or using a class of students to model your new range of clothes, again every child in the photograph must give you a signed consent form. If you don't insist on this, it will take the parent of just one child – who withholds permission – to invalidate your entire photo call. You will have invested time, effort, energy and money, and worse, you will have nothing to show for it.

Children reacting to something in an unexpected way can make great photos. Animals which were expected to sit at the foot of a child but which are now having their bellies rubbed by those same children make much better photos than the ones originally planned and posed. It takes more time, but the results can be terrific.

A good photographer makes all the difference too. You need to know who you are booking for the event. A photo call is an open invitation to media to attend and photograph, but you must always have your own photographer there so that (a) you have a record of the event and (b) you have professional photos to send to any media who could not attend.

So, what are you looking for in a photographer? Look at media photos that you admire and find out what photographer took them. Do not use photographers who are great at weddings, or food photography, or the friend of a friend just out of college. You have invested too much in this photo call – don't skimp on the photography, which is the most important element from a media perspective.

Photographers who work with companies, shooting photos for media, are often referred to as PR photographers. The media will know them and will trust them as a source of good photos. These photographers also keep an eye on the media on a daily basis. They will know if a similar style of shot has been used in the past few weeks and so will not be of interest to newspapers. They will also be used to dealing with celebrities and often know how to handle them! A good photographer can make all the difference to your event. Let me give you some examples.

I had a photographer at an event for senior citizens. Most people are shy about being photographed. When did you ever see a photo of yourself that you loved? (It seldom happens.) The first lady he asked declined to be photographed. Without batting an eyelid he immediately apologised and asked if her mammy knew she was at the event? The lady was in her mid-to-late seventies and loved the joke. She got his humour. He got his photograph and others joined in too. The photo call was very successful.

On another occasion, my photographer got the address wrong and arrived at the right address with around five minutes left before my three high-profile millionaire investors departed. The three, all men, had been waiting for ten minutes and were furious at the delay. They just wanted to give out to the photographer and leave. He arrived into the room, never apologised, but instead asked the first man if he was usually photographed looking to the right. The man replied that he was not. 'Well,' said my photographer, 'you should always stand on the left of a photo because your right is your best side.' He instantly had them looking for advice on how they should pose for photos. We got the shots we wanted!

By comparison, I sent a photographer to the home of a celebrity who was obliging us with a photo shoot. She was to be photographed at home and would lend her endorsement to a project my client was working on. (I cannot remember now why I could not attend, but I was not there.) The agreement was that the celebrity would be photographed early in the morning, as soon as the children had gone to school. I arranged for the photographer and a representative of my client to call to the house at 7.30 a.m.

When I telephoned the celebrity later to ask if everything went well she was not happy. My client, she said, was a lovely man who arrived into the house, recognised the usual morning madness and mayhem that is family life, and asked her could he make a cuppa in the kitchen. She really appreciated his approach. The photographer, on the other hand, told her that she was wasting his time and the client's money by not being ready – the children had not yet left for school and her husband was in a flap about something-or-other that he could not find. The photographer got her more stressed than she needed to be. The resulting photos were very good and very professional on her part, but they lacked the warmth that would have been there if the photographer had had more sense!

During a photo call a good photographer will take hundreds of photos in the space of 20–30 minutes and before they leave your function they will be able to show you (on camera or laptop) which photos they are submitting to the various media outlets. Photos are sent instantaneously to the media. So it is important that you have prepared a photo caption in advance that you can email to the photographer so that they can embed it into the photos being sent out. Your photo caption explains what was happening on the day. 'Pictured at the launch of the new XPQ range of garden equipment were (L–R) …'. Or 'Signing a Sino-Irish joint venture agreement in Cork were (L–R) …'. That way you control the message which accompanies the photos.

Always caption a photo from left to right, as this is the way the people look at photos – at least in the western world! Be sure that you get people's titles and the spelling of their names right. If it is a group photograph, you should caption it by naming the key person and the group, for example, 'Tom Jones pictured with members of the Palestrina Choir …'.

For media photographers attending the shoot, you should have a press release ready to give them. This release names the people (correct spelling and titles) who will be appearing in the photos. You should also take note of what media take which photos. If one of the papers is running late to the function they will ask you what shots the other papers took and will expect you to know.

Sometimes, by the nature of the photo call, all the media will get the same type of shot. This might happen if it is the signing of an agreement, for example. But the opening of a new factory would allow each newspaper to get photographs in different locations and possibly using different people. Your job is to make it as easy as possible for the media to get the photograph that they want.

Watch the dignity of the people you are inviting to be photographed. A shot of the guest of honour with feet outstretched, showing the holes in the soles of their shoes might get great coverage in the papers, but it is not something that you would issue from your company. Similarly, an unflattering shot of a thin man showing the extra weight he is carrying on his stomach, or highlighting a bald patch that is usually covered, might well be deemed to be 'quirky' by the media – but you would not issue it. You cannot, however, prevent these photos being taken. You have invited the media to take pictures and it is entirely up to them what they choose to photograph. They will select the photos that they think their readers will find most appealing. You will have to roll with the punches on this one – and probably be very grateful for the resulting publicity!

When the photo call is over, try to maximise the benefit of the visuals. Look at the different media – traditional and online – that you can issue photographs to.

Think of sending them to bloggers with your press release, see if you can put a selection up on your Pinterest account, create a photo album on your Facebook page, pop them into Google+ and tweet them to followers. You should also select some for the office wall or the next corporate brochure. The law, by the way, is very interesting in this area. The photographer, to the best of my knowledge, actually owns the copyright of the photographs – they are their creation – but because they were paid to create them, they may not use them (for example, by submitting them for competition or by selling them to someone else) without the permission of the person who commissioned them and paid for the service.

Depending on the arrangement you reached with the photographer, they will either give you a disc with all the photos or a selection of the photos on it, or they will put the contact sheet (a selection of miniature photos) onto a controlled website to which they will give you access. You can then select the agreed number of photographs, which will be sent to you or issued to the media on your behalf. You should issue to national print and social media on the day. You will issue to magazines afterwards.

Photo size is important. Your photographer will take pictures in the largest possible megabyte size. Large sizes are needed for the print media – and extremely large sizes for glossy magazines – to ensure good quality reproduction.

In contrast, you need a very small size (often less than half a megabyte) for social media.

What happens when the photo arrives in to the picture desk? It will be looked at for a matter of seconds and someone will decide if it has potential or not. If the answer is 'not', your photo will not see the light of day in that media outlet. Even though the photo was only seen for seconds, a trained photographic eye will remember that they have seen and rejected it, so there is no possibility of you reissuing the shot again a few days later.

You should send the photos to the daily print media on the day that the event happens, but the Sunday papers will take photos up to the Thursday lunchtime before publication. If your photo call is early in the week, this allows you to issue different photos to the Sundays, which will either maximise your media spread (if you have already achieved coverage in the dailies), or give you a second chance to get some coverage if you were unlucky earlier in the week.

And finally, remember that photographs have a short shelf-life. They date very quickly. Make sure that you get the most from them while they are current. By next week, the government might have fallen, the celebrity might have been dumped from the soap opera, or the team might have been knocked out of the competition. All of these events make your news 'old'. Use the photographs as quickly and as cleverly as you can and, whether you paid your participants or not, send them a souvenir photo and a thank you note. It costs nothing – and you never know where it might lead.

CASE STUDY – THE BUTLER'S PANTRY

This case study is based on an interview with Jacquie Marsh, managing director of The Butler's Pantry.

The Butler's Pantry describes itself as a provider of home cooking: 'We cook the way you would at home, with a generous spirit and using only the very best of fresh, natural ingredients. At The Butler's Pantry, we make all our food by hand and from scratch in our own kitchen. We rely on the finest ingredients, and we don't use additives and preservatives, so our food has a shelf-life of just a few days. Our menus are short and change with the seasons. The talented chefs and bakers in our kitchen are privileged to work with an abundance of wonderful Irish produce,' they say.

The company has been around since 1987. It has 100 employees. There are ten shops. During the recession they adapted their business model so that they could offer products at an acceptable price-point, although their core products never changed and never decreased in price. They are now re-positioning back to where they were – providing a premium-level product.

Photography is crucial to the business. They use it a lot for menus, point of sale, promotional flyers, web pages and social media. They divide their photography into two different categories, which are, roughly, merchandising and media.

MERCHANDISING PHOTOGRAPHY

Most of their merchandising photography is done in-house. They have no photographer or stylist on their team, and they don't have a marketing manager either. They have an in-house team of two people who are largely responsible for the merchandising photography, which is shot by a staff member. These people trial and test extensively before they take their photos, helped out by some of the other staff members. An in-house manager in one of their shops, who is a former architect, has a really good eye for structure. A couple of other staff members, who are foodies, are into merchandising and styling, and their head chef is especially good at styling photographs. This is the creative team that Jacquie Marsh works with in-house.

The team tries to style the food (she says they 'prop' the food) to fit with how people will use it. If the food is for a round-table family meal, they will style it in a kitchen. If it is food for entertaining, they will 'prop' it like that; if it is for picnics it is styled outdoors, etc. In one case they had to do a photo shoot for a promotion of salmon barbecued on a cedar plank. The photo shoot was done in Jacquie's back garden. The result was a quirky photo that went down very well with food bloggers and tweeters.

The company creates a huge volume of print material each year. They produce two to three product lists annually and photos are an essential part of these. Each of their product lists has a print run of 10,000. Jacquie estimates that as much as 25–30 per cent of their marketing budget is spent on photography.

MEDIA PHOTOGRAPHY

Photos for the media, however, are a whole other ball game. Jacquie believes that if you are not using a registered photographer, who is known to the newspapers, you have no chance at all of getting any coverage. There have been occasions when newspapers have sent photographers out to them, but that was usually when the paper had approached them to do a feature and was the original point of contact. In such instances, the media usually knows exactly what they want the photo to look like.

For the media, Jacquie stresses that you need to be very clear about what you want from particular shots. The photographer won't be able to get the shot if they don't understand exactly what you are looking for. Good input from you will create good output from them. Give clear direction. Jacquie has actually drawn pictures as part of a brief to a photographer, to show them exactly what she believes the photos should look like. Her advice is that you should find the creative idea first – then find the press photographer and make them understand exactly what you need.

The Butler's Pantry always sets up a few different versions of the photos they are looking for two or three days in advance of the professional shoot, to make sure that they are getting the 'look and feel' that they want. They believe that if you are spending around €1,000 for a professional photographer, you have to know what you are getting for it. It's too much money for a small business to waste.

They also try to get some newsworthiness into their photos. When they opened a new shop in Castleknock, for instance, they set up a photo that included John Hempenstall, who produces their buttermilk, Niall Hill, their executive chef, and Bobby Kerr, because of his connection with small business and the programme he had at that time on Newstalk.

The team puts a lot of thought and effort into every photo. They don't have a marketing budget for advertising, so PR is extremely important to them. While they have used both external and internal PR, in 2011/2012 budgets dictated that external PR had to stop and so now they do a lot of their PR in-house. Guerrilla marketing and media ambassadors work well for them. They regularly refer to media ambassadors – journalists who like covering their stories. As a business they are lucky because they are good at coming up with silly ideas and as a result they get product mention or a 'thank you' on air.

A good example of their guerrilla marketing comes from a few years ago, when they knew that a celebrity, one of their media ambassadors, was having a fortieth birthday. They figured, correctly, that everyone would concentrate on the day of his birthday or the time immediately around that. They decided not to. Instead, they focused on the six-month anniversary of his birthday. Cleverly, they baked him half a cake, and sent it to him wishing him a happy 40.5 birthday. His researcher said that he was on the floor laughing – he thought it was hilarious. As a result, he thanked them on air for the present and they even made it onto the 'playback' programme at the weekend. That's good PR.

Another example of this type of marketing revolved around the manager in their Temple Hill shop. She and her husband entered a wife-carrying competition in Lithuania or somewhere like that. They came tenth, but that didn't matter. The Butler's Pantry decided to issue information to media saying that anyone entering the wife-carrying competition the following year should be eating their sourdough bread. That one landed on Lyric FM!

JACQUIE'S ADVICE ON PHOTOGRAPHY

- A picture really does tell its own story. It is very powerful.

- Don't be afraid to test it in-house. Practise it. Trial it until you think the picture works.

- If you are retaining professional photographers be very clear about how you want the product to look and what the function of the photo is. If you can paint the picture in the photographer's head, they will capture it on film.

WHAT WORKS FOR THEM?

- Photos of awards.

- Photos of the opening of a new store.

- Incorporating some of the professional photographs into their product lists, which are available in-store.

- Taking something quirky – like the photo they got of one of their bakers being chased by the chef! That photo is three years old and will continue to be used for another few years yet. It was professionally taken to go out with a press release.

- Using the photos on their web page and on social media. Although their profiles show that the majority of their customers are over forty-five, social media has become an increasingly important publicity tool for The Butler's Pantry. In the last two to three years the time they have invested in social media has increased exponentially each year – but that's because they were starting from nowhere.

5

SPONSORSHIP

Sponsorship is a great way to create name awareness and to reinforce your presence in a particular market. When people think of sponsorship they think of the major sponsors – Discover Ireland for the RDS Horse Show for example, or the Permanent TSB Ideal Home Show, or Dubai Duty Free for the Irish Derby. These sponsorships are superb – they attract TV coverage and show what good sponsors can achieve with the right connections, but they are also extremely expensive. Moreover, companies like these have large teams of people who work on sponsorship only and the cost of the sponsorship can be easily evaluated in terms of return on investment.

For most SMEs this level of sponsorship is out of their reach. However, most have a promotion budget that could, and possibly should, be spent on sponsoring something which brings the business to the attention of the wider public.

Let's begin by separating out sponsorship from do-nation. A donation is charity – giving money to a good cause. Don't look for anything in return. Give it because it makes you feel good. You could possibly create a fixed fund each year to be donated to 'good causes'. You might also create an employee committee to decide who should receive some charitable donation from your business. It is a nice way of helping deserving causes.

Sponsorship, on the other hand, is an investment – it involves giving money, but in return you get a quantifiable commercial gain from your investment. So if you have a few bob to spend and want to sponsor an event so that you can raise awareness of your business, where do you start?

Let's look at who you are trying to reach. Do you want to be better known within your local community? Maybe you want to develop a bigger presence among a particular age group because of a new product you are introducing? Perhaps you want to be better known and better branded to an audience of females in the thirty-five to forty-five age bracket. Maybe your target audience is parents, or people who sail, or residents' associations? Whatever the audience, you begin with them and then look for a sponsorship opportunity.

Once you have chosen your audience, you need to find out what it is into. At the very least you will need to do some desk research to establish what its interests are. For young people should you sponsor something in music or technology? For thirty-five to forty-five-year-old women should it be something in fashion, business or education? For the local community is it an event that is missing from the summer festival, or a clean-up of the local playground?

There is a lot of cross-over between sponsorship and CSR – corporate social responsibility – initiatives, so let me try to briefly explain the difference. Broadly, sponsorship is identifying an opportunity to create a presence for your business or product, which puts you in front of a target audience that you are seeking to reach. CSR might be a sponsorship, but the key objective is not publicity. In this instance, it is about enhancing the quality of life of the recipients of your CSR initiative.

Back to sponsorship. If you have a pet shop and a member of the local community approaches you and asks for a €200 donation to sponsor a dog walk, this would seem to fit nicely into a target audience that you might be seeking to reach. However, the €200 is hard-earned profit – so you should be sure that you get a return on it. Instead of saying either yes or no, you should find out more about the package on offer. So you might ask if it is possible for the walk to start or end at your pet shop. What kind of advance publicity is being planned? Will you be named as a sponsor in all of the press releases? Are they hosting a press reception to announce details? If so, will you be able to put some branding around the room? Will you be called on to say a few words? Can you leave a product sample or leaflets on the chairs to remind people about your business? For the walk itself, can you provide branded water-bowls along the route for the dogs to drink from? If walkers are wearing numbers (like athletes), could you also put your business name on those numbers? Are people congregating somewhere at the end of the walk? Can you make a speech thanking everyone for supporting the walk and your business over the years? How can you make sure that you get a good return on your €200 investment?

Very often charitable and voluntary groups look for sponsorship but what they are actually looking for is a donation – a present of money. They are holding an event for a good cause and they want money to help them run it. It is your job to educate them about sponsorship. They need to understand that €200 is as much money to you as it is to them if they took it out of their own pockets. With some negotiation, and a little responsiveness on both sides, everyone wins. In fact, it might be the start of an annual sponsorship for the group that you would be happy to continue.

The amount of money that you invest in the sponsorship should be calculated against the number of people you will reach. If you had fifty walkers in the example above, the cost to the pet shop is €4 per walker. Only you can decide if that is a good return on your investment.

If dog owners spend a lot of money with you, and you have the possibility of reaching new ones, it might be a great investment. It might also be a good investment if it reinforces your presence in this market. However, if dog owners are the lowest spending group who come through your doors, you might feel that sponsoring something closer to 30 cents each would be more appropriate.

Sponsorship, like everything else, takes time if you are going to do it properly. For example, again for the pet shop above, there might be an additional cost in creating branded water-bowls. The cost might be very small (the equivalent of putting Letraset on plastic bowls), but the return, the branding, the visibility, enhances your sponsorship and makes sure that you get more from it.

If you are actively looking for an event that might suit your company to sponsor, it is important to tailor the sponsorship to suit your particular line of business. For example, if you own a bookkeeping business, it would make sense for you to sponsor something for other businesses in the area. If you are a clothes retailer, you might look for a fashion show that you could sponsor.

You need to do some careful research here before you invest. This isn't about money – this is about reputation. What do you know about the organisers? If the group does not have enough expertise to run the function, or they are 'relaxed' about the details, you would be better not to sponsor. The last thing you want is for people to associate your business with a badly run event. Worse, you will certainly not have factored in putting a huge amount of time and staff into the event to make sure that it isn't a disaster! So choose your sponsorship partners carefully. They do not have to be commercial entities. Local organisations and voluntary groups that have been doing a good job for years will continue to do a good job. Just do your homework before you commit money.

Once you have decided to sponsor an event, figure out what you need to know. Let's take the example of a clothes retailer. If you are sponsoring a fashion show, will it be exclusively clothes from your store? Are other sponsors involved? Can you ensure that each sponsor covers a different area? If yours is daywear, other sponsors might be for workwear, evening dress or outdoor clothes. These would all complement but not compete with you. You do not want to sponsor something that has a direct competitor involved. The best example that I can think of where competing businesses might be involved in joint sponsorship would be for something huge, like the Olympic Games, where you could find both Pepsi and Coke involved. In a case like this, the cost of the sponsorship is simply too enormous for any one company to cover, and the viewership figures and attendance are far too large for a company the size of Pepsi or Coke to decide to abstain! However, it is highly unlikely that your SME will ever be involved in an event of that size.

Once you are sure there are no competitors involved, you need to look at how you can maximise your involvement in the sponsorship. Do you have an ezine which you issue? Can you tell your readers that you are sponsoring this event and encourage them to go along on the day? Can you put up posters in the shop or office to encourage customers and staff to get involved?

And what about the details of the arrangement? If the sponsorship is large, there will be a formal contract between the parties. But even if the sponsorship is small, there should be binding commitments on both sides. A contract is an exchange of letters, effectively, so can you detail, on paper, the terms that you have agreed with the organisation: where and when they will use your logo, what strapline they will apply to the end of every press release they issue, what events you will be invited to speak at, etc. Tie it all down in the early stages. It prevents a lot of disagreement afterwards.

Co-sponsorship can be difficult because inevitably one of the sponsors will be better organised, will possibly have their own PR company working for them and will generate good publicity for themselves from the event. Let's assume that you have agreed to co-sponsor a Christmas dinner for senior citizens. Yours is a local corner shop and the organisers have told you that it would not be right to allow you to put up any branding on the night because this has never been done in the past and the other sponsors are happy not to have it. What they are looking for is someone to give a fixed amount of money and maybe contribute a box of biscuits to the goody-bag that senior citizens get when they are going home. If you agree, and it seems perfectly reasonable, then you need to find a way of branding your biscuits so that your sponsorship is obvious to everyone who attends the event. Perhaps you will gift-wrap the tins and apply a specially printed card which says something like 'Merry Christmas to you and yours from everyone in Burkes Family Stores. Thank you for your business over the years. We appreciate it very much.' The cost of the biscuits is a fairly high expense (depending on the number of people attending) but the additional cost of the wrapping paper and card is minuscule. The impact, however, will be sizeable. Coming back to where we started from, if you are sponsoring you are looking for a return on your investment. That's one way of getting it.

As a sponsor you also need to determine how much of your time, or your staff's time, will be needed. It might be that the event organisers just need a financial commitment from you. Find out in advance so that you can schedule time! Are there any members of your business who might be interested in getting involved on the day? If the business is sponsoring something, it is always nice to involve staff members. They too should have pride in what you are doing.

Will you need to involve someone else in your sponsorship? For example, if you are sponsoring a glamorous granny competition, should you hire a well-known female celebrity of senior years to present the prizes on your behalf? Would it make for a greater impact at the event? The organisers would probably be thrilled. It will cost you a fair bit more than your original investment, but it might keep those glamorous grannies talking about you long after the event has ended. It is well worth considering.

Watch out for food and drink at events. Food nowadays is a minefield. People have all sorts of allergies and food intolerances and you need to be sure that if food is offered, there are alternatives available to cater to every need. You should also be certain that everyone knows the contents of every dish being served. You don't want someone to enquire only to be given the wrong information and perhaps become ill. That is not the kind of publicity you are targeting.

Similarly, you might be very generous with your budget for drink but you also have to make sure that you are socially responsible. Senior citizens could be going home to an empty house where no one can keep an eye on them if they are 'tiddly'. People in their mid-twenties might be going on to another function at which more alcohol will be served. Most organisations nowadays offer vouchers for drinks. These can be free and allow the bearer one or two free drinks. After that, they may purchase drink if they wish. This is not mean-spirited, it is a socially responsible approach. If someone is coming along just for the free drink, they will be disappointed. If someone usually has three drinks on a night out, they won't mind paying for one of the three. Try to think ahead to what could possibly go wrong and how it might impact on your business. You really do need to be able to see around corners sometimes!

While we are thinking of senior citizens, how will they get home after an event? Can you provide mini-buses to bring them to their doors? Will the mini-bus driver be instructed to wait until they see the person safely inside before they leave? These are all small things that you would probably instinctively do as an individual. For a corporate event, you just need to make sure that the instructions are written somewhere and nothing is left to chance.

Another type of sponsorship that you might consider is organising a local initiative. For example, you might sponsor something like the clean-up of a local playground. Let's assume that it is a private playground and needs a good tidy up and a lick of paint. If you own a hardware store, this might be a wonderful opportunity to do something for the community. You could provide workers – people love to volunteer to do something different – who would clean and paint the playground. In return, you might ask if a plaque could be erected saying that your business has sponsored the playground for a year. You might, on an ongoing basis, ask staff to keep an eye out and make sure that it is looking good any time they pass by, or set up a structure whereby locals can tell you if the area is becoming run down again or dirty.

This type of endeavour is certainly sponsorship. There is a cost to you even if you are not handing over any money to organisers. You are paying the wages of the staff involved in the clean-up and the paint is costing you money, even if it is at wholesale rates. So it is definitely sponsorship, but it might also qualify for a CSR award and you might choose to seek that type of recognition. There is no harm at all in doing good, for the right reasons, and being rewarded for it. Entering the awards competition will create a sense of pride among your staff. If you are shortlisted (even if you don't win), you can use it as an opportunity to thank them for their involvement and point out that others in your peer group recognised you for doing something worthy and of value to the community in which you work and live. If you win an award, you have even more to celebrate, as well as a publicity opportunity that you didn't set out to create but which will ultimately be of benefit to your business.

CASE STUDY – ACTION COACH

This case study is based on an interview with Paul Fagan, Business Coaching Ireland, who is the master franchise owner (Ireland) of Action Coach. Paul bought the franchise in 2010 and has spent the years since building a team and building his business.

Action Coach holds seminars and workshops for AIB, and runs about fifty management works courses each year. These courses target SMEs who want to build their businesses. The company has an impressive track record and achieves enviable results. The overall impact on businesses or the business owner participating in coaching or training is 99 per cent positive. In 80 per cent of cases, businesses report increased sales where their competition is static, and an impressive 68 per cent report an increase in profitability. Although not targeting job creation per se, the result of profitability is an increase in sales, which usually leads to job creation. One-third of the companies that Action Coach has worked with have created jobs as a direct result of their coaching. That's an impressive 300 new jobs in the economy arising from the work of this small company, with each new job estimated to be worth €15,000 net to the exchequer.

Action Coach's headquarters has been in Ballymun since the company opened. It has a sponsorship initiative that it calls 'coaching for a cause'. Each of their coaches works pro bono, giving coaching sessions to businesses or individuals. These businesses or individuals might be referred by a colleague, or they might directly approach Action Coach looking for help as they lack the funds to pay for professional coaching. As part of 'coaching for a cause', coaches work on a one-to-one basis with businesses, helping them to gain clarity around what they are doing. The job of the coach, according to Paul, is to ask lots of questions in order to establish exactly what the problem is (a bit like a doctor). Often companies are looking in the wrong place when they are seeking solutions to problems. The coach's job is to shine a light on other aspects of the business and help companies to identify and tackle problem areas.

It's a very clever sponsorship idea. The return on investment for Action Coach is that they get the benefit of working in the business community 'below the radar', helping businesses to grow, develop and thrive, businesses which in turn recommend their services. Also other local businesses watching their competitors see the benefits that this coaching delivers and avail of it for themselves. So, this quiet 'coaching for a cause' generates new business and positive feedback for Action Coach on an ongoing basis, and ensures that their company is associated with business success.

Action Coach has been doing this pro bono work since the company started. One of the clients they work with is Philly McMahon, the well-known Dublin GAA footballer. Philly is from Ballymun and runs a small gym in the area. Action Coach has been working with him for the last year or so. Philly is an enthusiastic supporter of Action Coach, crediting them with giving him the ability to reap better business rewards and play better football because of his new focus. He says that their coaching has brought clarity to his business and allowed him to find the space to concentrate on playing for Dublin. In 2015 he was named on the GAA GPA All-Star Football Team of the Year and was shortlisted for Player of the Year.

Philly has also set up a scholarship in memory of his brother, who died of a drug overdose. The scholarship gives one or two young people each year the chance to train as fitness coaches, which, once they have qualified, allows them to work as fitness instructors. It is a skills-based initiative, which Philly believes will help children in the Ballymun area. Action Coach attended a fundraiser for this event in The Cube. They sponsored a table of guests and donated money, but they also decided to work more closely with Philly to see if they too could sponsor an initiative for the local community of which they are a part. The result is a new CSR initiative called 'Growing Business. Supporting Communities.' It was launched in November 2015 and it, too, targets young people in the area.

Action Coach is working with transition-year students from the local Trinity Comprehensive School to teach them basic business skills, improve their self-confidence, restore some self-esteem and hopefully make them more employable when they leave school. The coaching starts with an online business health check which the company has on their website. They have adapted this for transition-year students so that they can establish their level of knowledge and business savvy at the start of the programme.

The coaching then gives students a basic business education by using a board game. The game, developed by Action Coach, teaches them how business works. It's a bit like Monopoly and offers participants choices about everything from increasing sales to investing in property and learning to handle ethical issues. The coaching gives students skills in the five main areas where businesses need to succeed:

- Lead generation (how to get business in).

- Conversion rate (how to sell to customers).

- Numbers of transactions per customer (which is all about creating loyalty).

- Average spend (what is the wallet share?).

- Margins and profit.

Action Coach believes that the course will have two major benefits for participants. The first is in the area of personal development, as it will help students to establish personal goals. It will teach them the art of goal setting and will empower them to visualise their lives in the future through use of a vision board or dream chart. It will improve their self-image and self-esteem, and will teach them the difference between self-worth and net worth.

The second benefit will be the business skills that participants acquire over a six-month period. Some of the graduates might decide to go into business for themselves. Others will have made themselves eminently more 'employable' because of the business acumen they have acquired. They will be thought of as an employee with a heightened awareness of how the business world works.

The evaluation of what they have achieved at the end of the programme will be done in two ways. The quantitative evaluation will revolve around the online business health check. Students who have taken this test at the start of the programme will be asked to take it again at the end. This will establish the level of improvement in their knowledge of business over the period of the training.

The qualitative evaluation will revolve around feedback from the students, their parents and teachers. This is feedback about perceived changes in attitude, expectations, dreams and aspirations. 'If we can change the lives of one or two children with this programme we will have been extraordinarily successful,' said Paul Fagan.

The company intend that this will be an annual CSR initiative targeting the community in which they do business. There is no cash outlay involved. What it requires is an investment of time and expertise, pro bono, in the students of the local comprehensive school.

6

NEWSLETTERS AND EZINES

I'm a fan of newsletters and ezines as I think they reach a different audience to social media. A newsletter is a physically printed object, while an ezine is the electronic version.

Ezines are for people who like their information to land into their inbox. They especially work for people who are forty plus in age, as those below that age often get their information from Facebook and Twitter. Nowadays most companies use ezines if they are issuing information in newsletter format. Ezines are not selling tools – their purpose is not to push sales. In their purest form, they are to provide people with information about your business. Nothing more. People who want to know more about you and your industry read them. They are targeted to a specific audience and perform a particular function.

Let's look at how you get started.

Building up an email list to send your ezine out to can be quite difficult. There are lists which you can buy, but I would not recommend them. Most of the email distribution platforms forbid their use, many of the email addresses listed appear to have been entered without permission (most are info@ or enquiries@ or sales@) and no one on a purchased list has shown any actual interest in your business. You are trying to target people who want to know more about you, so you need to begin by gathering their email addresses.

I am working on the basis that your ezine is targeting actual and potential customers. You can have a separate ezine for staff. In fact, email is so cost-effective, you can divide your audience into several different categories and produce a different ezine for each. However, let's concentrate for now on the ezine for customers.

It is imperative that you ask people's permission to put them on a mailing list. Database rules are strict on this. You cannot just trawl the Internet for email addresses and then start mailing people. It is rude, ineffective and illegal. To start collecting addresses, you might put a 'sign-up' button on your website, or ask people at an exhibition if they would be interested in receiving your ezine. You will also find that once your staff become aware of the fact that you are looking for email addresses, they will help in gathering them. I was in a new hairdressers recently and when I was paying the bill the girl said, quite casually, 'Oh, and I need your name, email and mobile please.'

'Why?' I asked.

'We always ask people for them,' she said.

The girl may or may not have known what it was for. I presumed – perhaps wrongly – that it would be for special offers. While I had no interest in hearing from the hairdressers again, I mentally commended the business owner for training their staff well.

If you gather people's addresses it is also important that they can choose to unsubscribe at any time. Most distribution systems include a button on each email that you issue, which says 'unsubscribe' and automatically takes you off the mailing list. Logically, you want this button to be there because, if for any reason someone no longer wants to hear from you, you certainly don't want to annoy them by sending them further information.

A few years ago a colleague of mine was receiving unsolicited ezines. She clicked the unsubscribe button when the first one arrived (she had no memory of ever signing up to it). A month later another arrived. She emailed the company to tell them that she had unsubscribed. They replied that it can sometimes take a few weeks before the request is actioned. A month after that she got her third ezine. She was so annoyed that she contacted the database commissioner to find out how she could report the company. As luck would have it, she was addressing a conference that same week about social media and the company which was mailing her was listed to attend. As part of her presentation she railed against this company, giving just enough information so that people could identify them, but not naming them. She concluded by saying that she had registered a complaint. The following morning she received a phone call from the company's MD saying that she hadn't been present the previous day but several colleagues had contacted her to tell her the story. She was ringing to confirm that my colleague's name had been deleted from the list.

Now I have to be honest. In my humble opinion, life is too short to get bothered about something like this. I would just hit the 'delete' button and forget about it ten seconds later. However, I completely accept that people have a right not to receive information that they don't want. And I don't understand businesses that don't use a distribution system which offers the recipient the option to unsubscribe and automatically deletes them from the mailing list. It is not something which needs to involve a human!

Mind you, I unsubscribed from an ezine recently and a lovely woman from the company phoned me a few days later to ask why I had unsubscribed. (It was actually because I subscribed to get information about the business in advance of a radio interview I was conducting with her boss.) She said that they always rang people because they wanted to know if they were giving the wrong information or if the information arrived too frequently or too infrequently. It was very clever. The customer was gone, but the company wanted to learn from it before they lost another one. I like their style.

So, you've decided that you are going to gather email addresses and mail people on a regular basis. Now you must decide how often this will happen – it really comes down to time. The cost of distributing ezines is quite small and the photography can be bought quite reasonably. What takes the time is deciding on the content and then writing it up. That can be very time-consuming, but once you have told people that your ezine issues every quarter, then it should actually do that. After all, you have now committed to it. So you need to think carefully about how much time is involved and how often you will be able to do the work involved in composing your ezine before you announce how often these will appear.

Next you have to decide what the ezine will contain. What kind of information will you carry? Do you have a schedule of pre-arranged functions or launches that you can work from so that you are sure you don't miss anything? Will you do a profile piece each quarter? If so – who will be profiled? If you agree that the directors of the company will be profiled, and there are six of them, what are you going to do in eighteen months' time? Your resource is finite. You need to be sure that when you start with a format you will be able to stick with it. Otherwise your ezine will look erratic and you will lose readers.

What style of writing will you employ? This may well be decided by the industry you are in. If you are in a legal firm, for example, your clients will probably expect quite a formal structure to your stories, some serious content and almost an essay style of writing. If your business is a playgroup for children, or makes children's toys, your audience will expect something a little zany, wacky and fun. If you are a service provider – like a graphic designer – your audience will probably expect hints and tips about the use of white space, new research about what colours to use, information about new trends in the business, etc. And, of course, the style should reflect your company ethos. If you are a serious, formal company, your ezine should be the same. If your company style is informal and friendly, that too should be reflected in your ezine.

How many articles will appear in each edition? This kind of detail is important. Will you always have one article by the CEO? A 'welcome' piece which also gives a corporate overview of how the business is doing or how the industry is changing because of European regulations or legislation. Let's assume that is one of the articles.

Your second article might be about your products. Be careful here – how many products do you actually have? If you have thirty and create four or five new products each year, then you are unlikely to run out of things to talk about. If, however, you have a limited number, you might look at approaching this topic differently and perhaps focus on the things people use your products for. This would give you much greater scope.

Your third article might focus on what your MD or management team are doing – books they have written, presentations they have been asked to give, awards they have won, industry bodies they have been elected onto, etc. All of this enhances your customer's knowledge of the business and reinforces their belief that you are an industry leader.

Your fourth and final article might be a quiz or a caption competition. You would like to know if people are reading your ezine, so putting a competition into it somewhere will encourage interaction, and it also gives you a prize winner and a new challenge each time your ezine issues.

Photographs are also important. Visuals are crucial – so make sure to use good ones. You can have photos taken specially for the ezine. You might, for example, have a photographer come into the business and take head and shoulders photographs of the entire team so that you have a really good photo on file for the next time you write something about them. You may also have professionally taken photographs of awards that you sponsored or received. You should definitely have high quality photographs of your product range, as you will need these for sales purposes anyway. The photographs that you use will be small in measurement and small in pixel size (half a megabyte or less), but this does not mean that you can use poor quality ones. A badly taken, blurred or distant photograph which looks bad in a large size will look just as bad in a small size. Don't use it!

You can buy photos from numerous photo agencies online. They vary hugely in price depending on the agency and the use of the photo. As a general rule, buy photographs for any stories that you do not already have a visual for. These can be simple words, for instance 'Success', clever cartoons, or photographs of people in a meeting. These photos are always bought in the smallest size available (XS) for use in ezines. Remember that some photos will be for editorial use only, so read the notes carefully. If you are likely to want to use the same visual in an advertising campaign, choose another so that your style is consistent and you are operating within the terms of your purchase agreement. Be conscious of your budget when you are choosing. You can pay anything from a couple of euro to twenty-five euro for a photograph.

Who will write your ezine? You want a consistency of style and you need someone with an ability to write well. Perhaps you should consider having someone trained in journalistic writing skills. (Your advertising people will be great at writing sales text but remember, your ezine is about telling, not selling.) You might also look at sending your designated person on a grammar course. Watch for things like the person's ability to spell properly or use words in context. Your business will be damaged by sending out badly structured sentences or misspelled words. There really is world of difference between 'there', 'their' and 'they're'. Compliment is not the same as complement. Relative and relevant cannot be used interchangeably.

You need to create timelines for your ezines. Fix the publication dates a year in advance and work back from there. How far in advance will you need the text finalised so that it can be signed off for publication? How long will it take to find good photos to go with the text?

And of course, in the initial stages, you will need to allow time for someone to learn how to put the ezine together. What platform will you be using? If your distribution list is small, you can probably distribute it using your own email system. However, as the list grows, you will need to look at one of the email distribution systems, such as Constant Contact, VerticalResponse or MailChimp. These provide a distribution platform which prevents your ezine from being listed as spam (most email systems are sensitive to bulk distributions) and they also allow people to unsubscribe painlessly. (By the way – very few people actually do.)

Once your ezine has been issued, you should check the statistics. How many of the original number did you actually deliver to in the end? (Some will have unsubscribed, some will have bounced.) Of those, how many people actually opened the mail? Of those who opened it, which article received the most attention? All of the good ezine distribution platforms offer this facility. It is amazing what you can learn by studying the statistics. By doing so, a colleague of mine, who is responsible for producing a golfing ezine, knows that every time his ezine contains a special offer on, say, golf balls, there will be a higher 'open' rate and the special offer will have the greatest number of readers. It makes sense, then, to save the special offers for months when, traditionally, the ezine attracts fewer readers.

You go to a lot of trouble to create and distribute your ezine. It is not an advertisement, so you cannot count sales made against distribution costs. So how do you quantify its value? This is one of the most difficult questions to answer – and I don't have a pat answer for it. An ezine really serves as a reminder to people that you are out there, your company produces whatever your product is, and they should think of you if they are thinking of buying that product. The result might be that you keep your customers loyal to your product. The result might be that people will buy from you when they need that product – which might be a few years after you started sending them the ezine. The result might be that they are reminded to recommend you to others, based on the service you gave them years ago, but which they might never need again! In short, you will never know statistically, so you need to pay attention anecdotally.

A good example comes from my own work. Over the years I have spoken with a number of people who told me that they signed up for one of the Irish Academy of Public Relations' courses 'at last'! It is something they had been thinking about for the last four or five years and never got around to until, for some reason, when the ezine landed one particular month they decided the time was right. I can happily live with that. The important point is that they kept accepting the ezine when it wasn't particularly relevant to them, bought from us (and not a competitor) when they did decide to invest in their education, continue to receive our ezine and might recommend us to others in the future. The sale is an added bonus in the equation.

CASE STUDY – IRISH ACADEMY
OF PUBLIC RELATIONS

This case study is based on our experience of how we create content and distribute ezines for the Irish Academy of Public Relations, a private college specialising in communications education. The Academy's headquarters are in Dublin, with offices in London and New York. It is my 'day job'!

The Academy first introduced a printed newsletter in the 1980s when the cost of print was expensive. Full colour print was initially a step too far, so the newsletter was produced using spot colour. The distribution at that time was approximately 900 people. Fast forward to 2015 when the Academy issues 36,700 ezines each month. Let's look at why ezines work so well for us.

Our audience is quite homogenous but also quite diverse. The people who receive our ezines are people who have an interest in the communications industry generally and communications education in particular. The Academy teaches online courses in public relations, journalism, event management, radio journalism, mobile journalism, grammar and social media marketing. Courses are taught online across the world. We have graduates in over fifty countries. Our courses are taught in six languages. Our tutors are based in eleven different countries. Ezines are the most efficient and cost-effective way of distributing a lot of information to a widespread audience.

Let's look at it clinically. The Academy's English-speaking audience is made up of people who are mostly drawn from three regions: Ireland/Europe (euro zone), England/Asia (sterling) and America (US dollar). To cater to this English-speaking audience, we have created three different ezines, which issue each month.

The ezines all share core information. They always give details about the next online courses and when they are starting. They also share information about the benefits of doing a particular course, or a testimonial recently received from a graduate. Courses begin every four to six weeks and the ezine helps to remind people that if they have not done a course already, there is still time to start one.

The ezines also highlight the people who have been interviewed on the *Mediascope* programme, which I present on Dublin City fm each week. *Mediascope* targets issues of interest to people working in the communications industry. In the past, I have interviewed journalists about how the media covers issues like migrant deaths or terrorist attacks. I have spoken to tweeters, social media experts and industry leaders, worldwide, about changing trends in business. Tourism promotion initiatives, changes in lobbying and broadcasting legislation, and attacks on journalists and cartoonists have all been covered. I have talked with experts about which newspapers are changing focus, and what the future of sports sponsorship or exhibitions is. In fact, the programme covers just about anything to do with marketing, social media, public relations, journalism, event management or anything broadly related. *Mediascope* is broadcast on 103.2 fm, streamed and made available as a podcast, which allows global access to the show. The ezines make it easy for people to identify this resource, which is useful to their business.

The ezines also keep graduates and others informed about things that the Academy is doing, both nationally and internationally. For example, they covered the story of the creation of the Orient Planet Academy, a joint venture between the Academy and Orient Planet PR leading to the creation of the first online communications academy in the Middle East. They also covered a trip that myself and Nollaig Whyte took to Nigeria to visit Academy students at Dorben Polytechnic and to address the first National Event Management Conference in Abuja. More recently, they covered my appointment as chairperson of Dublin City fm in November 2015. The ezines also keep readers up to date about the Academy's involvement with the annual Irish Bloggers Association's Blogger Choice Awards, the DubWebFest, the Beca Pilosof Award and other conferences and events that the Academy is involved in.

The Academy's courses are mostly online, but we physically teach two skills – radio and television presenting – in studios in Dublin. The ezines remind people about their next opportunity to acquire these skills, as well as sharing stories about the radio and TV tutors who teach our courses and the graduates now working in the industry.

This is the basic structure of our ezines. Each links back to a dedicated website for specific regions (the Academy has eight websites for each of the regions of the world that it currently serves) and each version also includes items specific to the area they are targeting. For example, the American ezine always contains a section called 'Broguery and Pishroguery'. For those who are not from Ireland, it is an opportunity to learn something about the psyche or history of the country. For those of Irish extraction, it is a link with the homeland.

The English ezine is also adapted for that market with an article each month of interest to UK-focused businesses, which might draw on examples from UK media or businesses.

In 2015 the Academy introduced a Spanish-language ezine. We had been expanding into Latin America and concentrating resources in that region. In addition, a dedicated website in the Spanish language had been created, as had a special Spanish-language Facebook page. It was time for a Spanish-language ezine. As well as sharing core content with our other ezines, this gives the Academy an opportunity to talk about the expansion of our range of courses in the Spanish language. It also profiles Spanish-language tutors who are giving presentations to conferences throughout Latin America, or special online presentations given to universities in the region. It puts a spotlight on Academy graduates and looks at how they are using their courses for the good of their communities or to enhance their careers. And, of course, it allows the Academy to cross-promote competitions we run on Facebook.

In the future the Academy is planning to develop ezines in Russian, French and Polish.

7

ENTERTAINMENT OPPORTUNITIES

We all like to be thanked. I was in the office one day when I met Cyril Stevens on the stairs. Cyril and his wife Vera run Lissadel Stationers and we had been buying from them for about ten years at this point. I asked Cyril why he was here and he explained that the girls had run out of envelopes and he was dropping a box over. I was absolutely mortified and apologised that we had given him a run from west Dublin to south Dublin with a single box of envelopes (quietly thinking that we really needed to review the way we order stationery). Cyril said that it wasn't a bother at all and, in fact, as soon as Vera told him that we were stuck he offered to drive the box over. After all, he said, when competitors came into the market and started hoovering up his clients we stayed with him. It was his way of saying thanks for the business. I never forgot it!

Organising an entertainment event is a great way of thanking your customers/clients. Let's look at the options that are open to you.

You should begin, as always, by looking at the people

you are going to entertain. What sort of interests do they have? This is not about you – it's about them. It doesn't matter that you love rugby if they are into soccer, or that you are a sports fan and they are into classical music. You are trying to entertain them in a way that they will find really memorable.

In a small organisation you will generally know what your clients are into – it can be more difficult in a larger business. But an SME will probably be able to tell you who is into movies, sports, travel, etc., based on the kinds of conversations they hold with their customers when they call into the office, or before a meeting begins.

You can always create an entertainment opportunity for your clients and sometimes this works really well. You might bring a small group out to dinner each year. You could book a private room in an upmarket restaurant (so that you are sure you will not be disturbed or overheard!) and arrange to have a quiet meal together. Good food. Good wine. Good company. All you need to add is a few words at the beginning of the night to explain that this meal is a way of saying thank you for all the confidence they have placed in you and all the business they have given you in the past year. After that – party time!

Many years ago, I was handling PR for the Kerrygold Dublin Horse Show. For the first show, An Bord Bainne – the new sponsors – were trying to figure out how to thank the media for referring to the show as the Kerrygold Dublin Horse Show. This planning was going on well in advance of the event actually taking place, and we all knew that a lot of work would go into branding the event and trying to make sure that the media used the sponsor's name when they were describing it. We were confident that they would do their best, so set about organising a thank you dinner. There was a lot of discussion about the best way to approach it. The event attracts an international cohort of media so you are dealing with multiple languages, multiple cultures and multiple tastes. In the end we settled on something uniquely Irish.

On the Thursday of the show week, we arranged for coaches to collect the media (as many as wished to attend – which was almost all) at the RDS grounds in Dublin. From there we travelled to Castletown House, an old and very large Georgian mansion on the outskirts of Dublin. We provided a sumptuous meal of the very best of Irish cuisine, plenty of wine and lots of Guinness and Baileys. As far as I can recall, we had little cards on the table thanking the media for using the reference (I don't think anyone actually made a speech on the night – but I could be wrong about that!). By the end of the evening, the Irish table was leading the sing-song, versus the German table and the Welsh table and the French table ... It was a wonderful evening. No pressure was applied to the media. No over-thanking was done either. It was just a great venue and a great opportunity to relax and enjoy each other's company away from the 'work' of the show. It was very well received.

I attended another function which was organised by Newstalk at Christmas. I contribute to their newspaper review on *The Sunday Show* occasionally and I presume that is why I was invited. On the afternoon of the event one of my colleagues rang to say that Newstalk had been in touch and wanted to know if I was staying for a meal. I was instantly plunged into a crisis. I told her there had been no mention of a meal on the invitation and I was planning to be there for just an hour or so (I had several functions to attend on the same night) and asked her to confirm that I would not be eating with them. How wrong I was! When I arrived, everyone was talking about the food. I HAD to eat, they told me. The food was just amazing. And it was. The portions were absolutely tiny but each meal was like a doll's version of a main course. I was served, for one dish, the smallest lamb chop I have ever seen in my life, on a bed of perfectly whipped potatoes (which would have fit onto a teaspoon) with teeny carrots. Absolutely fabulous. There were other dishes too – apparently there were five or six main courses and everyone, myself included, had one of each. There was a fish and chip dish, I recall, with a small portion of fish and a tiny ceramic dish, which looked like a cupped newspaper, with a very small portion of terribly skinny chips. Delicious. The event was to thank everyone for helping to make Newstalk such a success in the previous year. If I'm still talking about it, the food must have been good!

Another way of thanking your clients is to create entertainment opportunities around an event that someone else is sponsoring. You don't need to be involved in the sponsorship at all – you might just want to entertain your biggest clients in an effort to say 'thank you' for the business. If you think of any of the rugby matches, there are plenty of opportunities to entertain guests before and after, and to sponsor their tickets – entertain them in a corporate box – to say thank you. If your key clients like classical music, you can purchase tickets for a concert in the National Concert Hall and book the boardroom for a private food and drink function in the interval, or after the event has ended.

Charity fundraisers are a great way of entertaining clients while supporting a good cause at the same time. They are not – be warned – as lively as they used to be! At the height of the Celtic Tiger, my husband – the artist Tony Gunning – donated a painting to a charity event which was being held in the Druids Glen Hotel. Martin King from TV3 was the MC for the night. A lovely man, he was at our table and was quite sure that he could raise more money than the charity expected. He was right. He got tremendous prices for everything which was auctioned

(I think Tony's painting sold for about three times the reserve) and Martin even managed to sell his tie for €1,500.

Post-Celtic Tiger, these events are much tamer, but they are still a great way to entertain clients and say 'thank you'. There are many charity lunches and dinners, especially around Christmas time, which raise much-needed funds for very good causes. If it is a dinner, then people will expect to be away for the evening and won't mind if things run a little late. However, be warned, if it is a lunch they might view things differently.

I was invited to a charity lunch last Christmas by our accountants. Great idea. I would get to meet other clients of theirs and we would all be raising funds for a good cause. It was a women-only affair. The lunch was arranged for noon for 12.30. We all arrived at noon. One of the clever things the charity did, by the way, was ask people to purchase a star from the Christmas tree. I think the star cost €35 and you were guaranteed to get at least that value back in the goody bag which corresponded with the star you had chosen. This was a great way to get money from the guests for the charity (I'm guessing that most of the tables at the event were bought by corporates).

However, to say that the function ran late would be an understatement. I think we finally sat down to eat just after 2 p.m. Service was slow – or relaxed – depending on your perspective, and the meal finished at about 5 p.m. If the meal had started at 12.30, had been finished by 2.30 and I had slipped away at 3 p.m., I would honestly have left thinking that I had had a lovely afternoon and had been away for three hours. In the end, I left just after 5 p.m. feeling that I had just devoted five hours to lunch!

There are other options as well. If the group you are entertaining are younger and of a slightly wilder disposition, you might do something like arrange for them to go paintballing. This highly competitive sport brings out the killer instinct in people. If you have a competing team who are equally determined to win, it can provide a great afternoon's entertainment. A friend told me that he brought a team of people out paintballing one afternoon and after thirty minutes he interrupted the game and asked to speak to the team leader on the other group. He complained that the other group were hardly trying, while his team were 'killing' all around them. The opposing team captain explained that they had a limited budget and could not afford to splash as much paint as my friend's team. Fine, he replied, we'll pay for your paint as well. Now get serious and start paintballing. A great afternoon was had by all.

You might also look at creating an opportunity to bring people somewhere and have an expert on hand to explain in detail what the event or building or object is all about. If you have a group who are interested in fashion, for example, you could arrange a tour of the museum in

Collins Barracks with an expert who can explain the relevance of each of the different styles. The national gallery will also organise tours to show you their collection, and you can arrange tea and scones afterwards!

During culture night, I attended a tour of the Waterford Medieval Museum. The man who led the tour knew everything about all of the exhibits on display. He was utterly fascinating to listen to and held his audience captive. In fact, he was enjoying himself so much that a colleague had to call him away to attend another function. (He was supposed to have stopped the tour thirty minutes earlier.)

Recently, I arrived too early for an event that I was attending in the Stormont parliament building. A lovely doorman recognised the fact that I was really interested in getting a look at the chamber (a truly historic location) and finding out more about the building. He spent an hour explaining about the fire which gutted the chamber, the second chamber which was originally used as the upper house, the paintings, the system for press reporting and who sat where in the chamber. I was utterly fascinated.

Women's Little Christmas is celebrated each year in January and I had always thought of it as a private or family or girls' thing. I never actually associated it with corporate events. One year, however, HETAC (The Higher Education and Training Awards Council) invited all of the female heads of colleges, departments and schools who were their clients, to share Women's Little Christmas with their female HETAC staff in a restored Georgian building on Merrion Square. We were the only group in the building on the night and, after a tour, sat in the first floor dining room overlooking the square, eating a sumptuous meal and swapping stories with colleagues new and old. It was a lovely occasion and it was rare to have an opportunity to meet other women in a similar position to myself.

Entertainment opportunities are created – with a lot of time and effort – so that you can say thank you to a group of people who are important to the success of your business. The event should be relaxed and should ideally offer people an opportunity to network with those whom they might not otherwise meet. There is no quantifiable outcome for your business, but if client retention is important to you, then this is an area that is certainly worthy of some thought.

CASE STUDY – A FUNDRAISING LUNCHEON

This case study had some input from Brown Thomas.

In 2000 the Irish Society for the Prevention of Cruelty to Children (ISPCC) and Brown Thomas came together to create a fundraising luncheon. It has been running every year since.

The ISPCC opened its first branch in Ireland in 1889 (a little later than Brown Thomas, which opened in Dublin in 1848). They are both well-established brands. The ISPCC has ninety full-time staff members and a volunteer team of 600 people. They provide twenty-four-hour services to young people in Ireland. It costs €6–7 million each year to maintain these services, with very little statutory support. In fact, 80–90 per cent of all funds spent each year are fundraised. They also concentrate on spending their money where it is most needed – on services. For every €1 raised, 83c goes to service provision and promotion, 15c is spent on fundraising and 2c is spent on administration. It's a tightly run ship.

Brown Thomas (BT) is a luxury store, headquartered on Grafton Street with branches in Cork, Limerick and Galway. It stocks luxury brands like Gucci, Louis Vuitton, Chanel, Dolce & Gabbana and Ralph Lauren. Its clientele has a high disposable income and likes to buy established brands and labels. They belong to an exclusive group of people who mostly know each other. These people like to set trends and be ahead of the curve. They are not particularly interested in freebies or 'something for nothing'.

Caroline Downey, one of Ireland's premier fundraisers and someone I profiled in *Capital Women of Influence*, is passionate about raising funds for the ISPCC and for their Childline service in particular. A member of the ISPCC board and their president, she came together with Brown Thomas fashion director Shelly Corkery and ISPCC event manager Penny Dix to collaborate on an event that would celebrate the ISPCC and, at the same time, introduce the new season collections at Brown Thomas. The annual luncheon was born. It is now in its seventeenth year and is so firmly established on the social calendar that tickets are sold out a year in advance. Over 380 guests attend each year, including ISPCC ambassadors, long-term supporters of the charity, Brown Thomas customers and the media. Ticket bookings are generally taken for a full table of ten people and are purchased by corporates and groups of friends.

Tickets are priced at €135 per person. Brown Thomas also hosts a raffle at the event which raises approximately €15,000 annually. The occasion is predominantly sold on reputation and, each year, corporates and customers re-book for the following year's event. Brown Thomas itself also books eight tables. It uses the fundraising lunch to bring key customers together in one place, to see the latest fashion trends, mix and mingle with each other, be publicly associated with Brown Thomas and help a worthy cause at the same time. It is a great way to showcase and sell to existing customers, while also generating funds for a good cause.

The management of the event is a huge undertaking. Brown Thomas looks after the production and staging of the fashion show, organises the goody bags (an important part of the enjoyment of the day), works with its brands to secure prizes for the raffle and manages all PR elements around the event. All ticket sales are managed directly through the ISPCC, which also works closely with key sponsors.

The attendees are predominantly women, although there are some men in attendance each year. It is a glamorous event. Women attending know that society magazines will be present and photographing. The attendees are as glamorously dressed as the models on the catwalk!

Moët & Chandon have been a key sponsor of this event for a number of years and guests are treated to a champagne reception on arrival. Each year there is a celebrity MC who welcomes guests on arrival, as well as speaking on stage. Previous MCs of the luncheon include Laura Whitmore, Sharon Corr, Donna Air and Amy Huberman.

There's always a speech from the president of the ISPCC, Caroline Downey. This puts the event in focus for the attendees and reminds them that the purpose is to raise funds so that the ISPCC can continue to work with children and provide services as needed. Guests then enjoy a three-course lunch, and the highlight of the day is undoubtedly the Brown Thomas Autumn/Winter Season Launch Fashion Show. Over twenty models take to the catwalk, showcasing designer clothes from the Brown Thomas store for men, women and children. In all over 100 looks are modelled.

In the fifteen years that this event has been running, it has raised over €1 million for the ISPCC.

Corporates enjoy attending because it creates an opportunity for them and their guests to mix in a celebrity circle, contribute to a good cause, enjoy a pleasant afternoon and say 'thank you' to key clients who have contributed to the success of the business over the past year. It also gives them an opportunity to participate and enjoy, without the hassle of creating and managing the occasion.

The planning for the following year's event begins immediately after the current event has ended. Each year, Brown Thomas hosts a review meeting, discusses feedback and plans for the next year while everything is still fresh in their minds. In everything that they do at Brown Thomas, staff are always looking at new ideas and new ways of developing concepts. With any large-scale event, such as the ISPCC show, it is imperative that they maintain the prestige of the occasion, so this will play a role in deciding whether to expand the event to a larger audience in future years. They also closely monitor feedback from guests; they discuss what works, what they would like to see more of, they speak with the MC and the media that

was in attendance. This feedback is a vital first step for planning
a successful event for the following year.

8

EXHIBITIONS

Exhibitions are a great way of bringing your company to the attention of prospective clients. They offer you an opportunity to reach an audience of people who have already indicated, by their very attendance at the exhibition, that they are interested in the product you are offering.

Exhibitions can be very costly, however, when you add the costs of the stand, personnel and print material together. So, for a three-day period and a large outlay you want to be sure that you get the biggest bang for your buck.

There are exhibitions which are purely business-to-business. These require a lot of organisation but generally are not labour or cost intensive. For the purposes of this chapter, I'm going to concentrate on public exhibitions.

If you look at something like the Holiday Fair or the Ideal Homes exhibition, you will immediately be aware of the community of interest that exists around these topics. Thousands of people attend each year to find out what the newest trends are, see what holiday destinations have been added since last year, or find out if carpet or wood flooring is the latest fashion in interior decorating. They want to know about the 'in' colours, fabrics and furniture styles. They want to know about cruises in the Caribbean or the Arctic, or holiday villas in Italy, or walking the Great Wall of China. All of these people have paid money at the door to be sold to. That is what a public exhibition is all about. The audience is self-selecting and interested in the topic.

From your point of view as an exhibitor, this audience is like gold dust. You spend a lot of time trying to find people who are interested in buying your product. At a public exhibition you have an audience of thousands who are just that – interested. However, not everyone will be interested in what you are selling. People might be interested in flooring not furniture, or cruises not villas. Not everyone coming through the door will want what you are selling, but you will find that most are curious and some are very interested indeed. When people pay their money to get in to an event like this, you have no way of knowing who they are or what they want, so you need to put a bit of work into finding out that information.

So let's start at the beginning and see what decisions you need to take.

In the first instance, you need to decide if a particular exhibition is right for your company and your products. Once you know that the exhibition is hitting the right market, you then need to start your research in earnest. Find out as much as you possibly can. Check with the exhibition organisers to establish how many people attended the event the previous year and the year before that. Is the trend up or down? What was the average spend at the exhibition? How many exhibitors are returning for their third and fourth year? (If they are continuing to spend money then they must be getting a return on it.) What type of people attended the exhibition? What age group? Mostly men or women? How long was the average stay? The more you know, the better you can plan.

If you are happy with the information so far, then you need to start putting figures on it. How much will a stand cost? What size stand will you get for that money? Is there an option to go for a bigger stand? What is included in the price – are there lights, power points for laptops and TV screens, shelving, tables, chairs, storage space? You need to start looking at how much this package is going to cost you when all this has been added together.

If you know these figures, you also need to look at what your competitors are doing. You are unlikely to be the only person in your particular niche who is exhibiting at this event. In fact, it might be a bit worrying if you were the only one. Either you would be a genius and well ahead of the curve, or you have missed something that they all know!

Anyway, you might want to look at the size of your competitor's stand. Is it bigger or smaller? Will that make you look like the poor relation or the bigger company? Do you need to go that big? If you go for a large size, will you have enough information, posters and product to dress the stand properly?

Where exactly do you want to take the stand? Research shows that most people come in through middle doors and turn to the left. If your stand is near the door on the left you will be one of the first stands that they see. Is this good or bad? Are they more likely to stop when they are 'fresh' or less likely on the basis that there are a lot of stands to look at and they are not going to begin by looking at each one?

If you are on the right-hand side, will people be exhausted by the time they reach you and less inclined to stop and find out what you are doing? Or will they think, 'thank goodness, at last the product I was looking for'?

Should you take a corner stand? They always create the illusion of more space and you have greater visibility of people coming towards you from two different sides, and they can see you from both angles as well. Would that give you more options to sell?

If you are near the coffee area or a toilet you will have greater footfall than most areas in the exhibition hall, but will people be looking at your stand or just killing time waiting to get into the toilet? Will they sit and chat, oblivious to what is going on around them, or sip coffee while looking at the stands around the perimeter?

There are no right or wrong answers to these questions – but you should consider all of them and decide what is right for you, before you make a decision.

When you know your location, you need to begin designing the look of the stand. When you are standing in front of the stand, what are you looking at? Where will your corporate logo be displayed? Will you have products displayed on the back walls? Would you prefer to have posters there? Have the posters been created already? If they already exist, are they actually suitable for this exhibition? Would you be better to get new ones designed?

What will the corporate look be, by the way? Even if you don't have a corporate uniform, should you introduce one for the exhibition? Should everyone wear a red jacket and black trousers/skirt? It would give a uniform feel to the stand and look very professional. It might be better than having people arrive in whatever they would normally wear. If you are selling a clothes product – like Ralph Lauren polo shirts – make sure that the staff are not wearing another brand or an unbranded version of a polo shirt!

If you have visual media you can use, is there room for a TV screen at eye level or just above? How will it be mounted? Is there a power point nearby? Will the organisers allow visuals with sound? (Sometimes the repeating loop of a video drives other exhibition stand holders crazy, so visuals with no sound might be better.) Does the video that you have actually work without sound or would you need to put a text underlay – like subtitles – on the video before you use it?

What kind of furniture is provided? Will you use the white plastic circular table and foldable chairs, or will you bring the mahogany table from the boardroom with some leather chairs? Will you need a comfortable couch and individual seating? What atmosphere are you trying to create on the stand? Is it strictly business, or are you trying to say quality, five star, relaxed, come and chat? Different styles will suit different businesses.

What else do you need besides furniture? Will you need a plant for the corner of the stand? Or will you dress the stand in an entirely different way? If you produce or sell outdoor clothing, for example, will you dress the stand like the face of a mountain, dress your people in casual adventure-wear, and use dummies suspended from ice-picks on the back wall to show off the clothing range? Remember that you are trying to entice people to stop at your stand. They are already in the hall. You need to make sure that they don't pass you by.

What about display stands? If you are showing

jewellery, you might need flat glass cases to display the goods. The cases might need to be capable of being locked at the back to prevent robbery. Will you be bringing those cases from the jewellery store that you run? If so, will the shop look denuded while you are at the exhibition?

What about paper? What kind of information and material do you want to give people to take away? Will you produce a single sheet flyer with photographs of your products and a web address for further information? Should you actually produce small (or large) brochures with detailed information about your entire range? Should you create a range of flyers so that people can take little, light flyers, DL-sized brochures, or detailed full A4 catalogues? How will people access this information? Will all of the brochures be on a public counter for people to help themselves, or will the catalogues be behind the desk and given only to people who are seriously interested?

What about the people who will be on the stand for the few days of the exhibition? Are they sales trained? There is no point in putting them there, willing to help, if they have no ability to either sell or gather useful information for the sales team to follow up on.

A good example of this, although not from an exhibition, was when I was changing my car a few years ago: one of my colleagues had a friend who owned a garage in Galway and suggested that he would give me a good deal if I bought from him. The next time I was in Galway the two of us went to the garage. Her friend wasn't there, but one of his salesmen took me out for a drive in the coupé I was interested in. When we got back to the garage I asked him what he would give me for the car I was driving, as a trade-in. He hummed and hawed and said that he would get back to me. I told him that I didn't live in Galway and was keen to tie this down while I was in that part of the country. 'Give me a ballpark figure,' I said. He seemed to think about it, but then reiterated that he would have to get back to me. I have no idea what was going on, or why he could not give me a figure on the spot – and I never got a follow-up phone call from him. As I ended up saying to my colleague, that negotiation was the equivalent of me standing on the forecourt with money in my hand saying, 'Please take this, I want to buy a car', and him refusing to take it. The chap couldn't sell water in the desert and was useless in the position of salesman. Needless to say, I ended up going elsewhere to change the car.

At an exhibition, you have a captive audience that wants to buy. So make sure that the people on your stand are capable of selling!

As well as making direct sales at the exhibition, it is important for future sales to gather information about the people who might be interested in your product. You need to find a way to get information from them. Can you offer a competition – a chance to win a prize if they enter their name, mobile number and email? The prize needs to be a good one to attract their attention and encourage them to enter. Remember that people are wary of giving you details that you might use for other reasons. You need to give them an option to tick on the form if they do not wish to receive further information from you in the future. You could also ask people if they are interested in signing up for your newsletter/ezine so that they will receive regular updates about your business and the industry.

What about the person who is handling PR for the exhibition? Can you get them working for you? If you book the stand early, the organisers will contact you early. You will be among the first group of people to receive information packs, requests for information about your stand and your products, etc. This is one bit that you should pay attention to, but most companies don't. Six or eight months out from the exhibition, you are being asked if you are doing anything special on your stand, if you will be launching any new products or inviting any celebrity guests. If you are organised enough and can give the exhibition PR people this information, you will get them working for you. They are looking for information that they can use to promote the exhibition. They don't particularly mind if they promote your business or some other. They just need interesting information, photographs and interviews to promote the exhibition as a whole. If you can give them the information, they will start working for you.

Also, check out who is opening the exhibition. These things are always planned well in advance and where the guest of honour stops on their tour of the exhibition is also carefully planned by the PR people to maximise the chances of gaining media publicity. So, before the event opens, someone will know exactly what stands the guest of honour will stop at, which route they will walk, how long they will speak for and how long they will be in the building. Again if you are organised early enough, and can create something of interest on your stand, you have as good a chance as anyone else of getting the guest of honour to stop at your stand. Look at things like props that would make a good photograph – if you are a barber can you offer them a mock haircut or better, have a barber-shop quartet sing to them (great for print, television and radio)? Can you get them to try on a deerstalker hat? Or play one of your guitars? Or put on a lab coat and look at your scientific experiment? The organisers will love you if you create something on your stand that will attract media attention, and they will make sure that your stand is on the guest's 'stop' list.

Finally, in terms of exhibition PR, there is always a press office at exhibitions. This is the area that press go to in order to gather material and decide if anything is worth a closer look. The press office contains information about the stands in general, and individual press packs from each exhibitor who submits them. These packs are freely available to the media and would generally be collected and brought back to the office or home to see if there was anything that was missed at the exhibition. So you need to put together a press pack for the event.

The press pack should be in a really nice-looking folder with your company name or product brand on the front. Inside you should have a press release with information about why you are exhibiting, how long you've been coming to this particular event, possibly the level of sales you generated last year, or the new product you are introducing to the Irish market at the fair this year. Give the media something to write about. You should also include photos in your pack. I'm a firm believer in the belt and braces approach, so I like to include printed photos and a CD or memory stick with the same shots. This just makes it easy to know what you are going to be looking at on the stick and encourages them to pop it into their laptop for a better view. It also means that the media have your photos to use (they need to be free of charge and you should state this) with whatever article they write about you.

How else can you attract this audience to your stand? Can you get a celebrity to visit? Is there someone connected with your industry that people would like to meet? Can you book them to attend at your stand for thirty or forty minutes? This is a great way of attracting media attention. But remember, if you do have a well-known personality, it is important to know what you are going to do with them when you get them to the stand. You might get them to try something on, or give a cookery demonstration, or speak.

Every exhibition has speakers. People love to hear experts offering an opinion, so they will often take time out to attend one of the talks given during the exhibition. Do you have any expertise in your area? Would you be a good speaker on a topic related to your business? The art and antiques fair in the RDS in 2015 had a guest presentation by Ib Jorgensen. Very cleverly his presentation combined his early life in fashion design with his later life in art collection and sales. He attracted an audience of people who were fascinated by his knowledge of fabric and design and who were equally spellbound by his collection of paintings. I'm sure that most (like me) then visited his art gallery stand to check out what exactly was on sale. His company was already taking a stand at the exhibition but by having him speak as well they maximised their chances of attracting attention. Very clever.

So, to sum up, for exhibitions you need to think location, cost, celebrity, promotional material, staff, sales training, media attention, speaking opportunities, value for money and return on investment.

CASE STUDY – HIGH ROCK PRODUCTIONS

This case study is based on an interview with Seán McDonagh from High Rock Productions.

Brothers Seán and Niall McDonagh set up their business, High Rock Productions, in 2011. They are both actors who have been working in television and theatre for the last fifteen years. They are also Irish language enthusiasts who are 'go fliurseach as Gaeilge'. Seán has acted in *Ros na Rún*, and Niall presented *Neelo* on TG4 for two series.

They created High Rock Productions, their new venture, for two reasons. The first was that they are both married with young children. Seán has two children, Conall and Doireann, both under three years of age, and Niall also has two, Sorcha and Dara, both under five. They wanted to have more control over their work life and be able to work closer to home. They were also seeking more structure in their lives and wanted to create a steady stream of income.

The second reason was a change in the Leaving Certificate syllabus. It used to be that 20 per cent of a student's marks in Irish were awarded for the spoken language. A syllabus change increased this to 40 per cent. The brothers felt that none of the existing Irish books were specifically written to help teachers teach communication, and they knew that it would be a challenge to get students comfortable with the spoken word.

The first thing they set about doing was creating a new live show for students – *Cath Amach É* – which supported the change in the Leaving Cert syllabus. As part of the syllabus, students are given twenty sets of pictures to prepare. On the day of the exam, they get only one to talk about. The show that the brothers created is a crazy comic take on all of the sets. In the four years that they have been doing it, they have perfected the art of involving people in the show and the related workshop. They learned tricks from street theatre and are always interactive.

In their first year, they wanted to book twenty schools. They got seventy-five. Word of mouth was incredible. In their second year, they were asked to present at the annual conference for Irish Teachers – Tionól Teagaisc. They actually did part of the show and involved the teachers, so that they understood the experience as much as the learning outcomes. Now in their fourth year, the brothers book about 120–130 shows per year and they are, they think, at capacity.

The brothers love being in control of their own work. It means that they have the ability to change things if something isn't working and they say, because it is their company, they always get the part!

EXHIBITION TIME!

In 2015 they introduced a new workshop – *Scéal* – for transition-year students, and they participated in a new exhibition for the first time. *Scéal* had been two years in development and it is a very different project. It begins with a short sketch, which runs for 10–15 minutes and they describe as 'bright, physical, with a little interaction'. After this, the students are divided into groups and given scripts to work on. Each group gets different sections of the script. The students work on the presentation of their lines and learn how to speak in Irish with confidence. At the end of the workshop they do a version of the show. Everyone is involved – there are twenty-six parts in the play.

As they were introducing this new workshop, they came across a transition-year exhibition called TY Expo, which was actually being held for the first time. The event ran over two days, 15–16 September 2015, in The Hub, Cillin Hill, Kilkenny and was aimed at TY students and teachers.

The timing was bad for them. The months of September and October are always spent in intensive rehearsals for the national tour of schools, which happens from November to March. However, they decided to take a stand and see what happened. Their decision was prompted by the fact that teachers are a difficult group to communicate with, as they are not on phones during the day, and while some are good at reading emails, others are not. They had found, when dealing with the fifth- and sixth-year student courses, that their best method of contact was by post. They post brochures to schools every year, which are a vital marketing and promotion tool for them.

So, having decided to take a stand at the exhibition, they

then needed to create a stand. They brought some puppets, which attracted attention but also encouraged interaction. There are some simple things that anyone can do with a puppet, so the students interacted with them as soon as they reached the stand.

They also used 'props' very cleverly. For example, they played tennis with an imaginary/invisible ball (and included sound effects). The children were reminded to bounce the ball twice before they served and they had to retrieve it when it went out of play. Even the security guard at the exhibition got involved, asking people not to walk on the tennis court and stand back while students served the ball! They attracted a huge amount of attention over the two days and their stand was constantly busy. They learned some valuable lessons too:

1. Gathering information

On the first day they gave out all the brochures they had brought with them, which was terrific and showed a great level of interest from the attendees. However, they soon realised that they had no idea which people had taken their brochures. They needed to get details from them.

So, on the second day of the exhibition, they decided to put up a sign-in sheet and ask people to give their name, school, email address and contact number. This allowed them to create a database of people that they could then use to follow up with teachers and send more information on to them. Curiously enough, they found that when one person filled in all four categories of information requested on the first few lines, others continued to fill in all the sections as well. However, once someone broke the cycle and, for example, didn't give a mobile number, then others followed suit and didn't give a mobile number either. Once they realised this was happening, they kept a close eye on the sheets. If someone didn't give their full information, they either wrote in details for a couple of lines beneath (to start people completing all the sections again) or started a new page. Very clever!

2. Resources on the stand

Even though there were two of them on the stand, it was sometimes difficult for people to get to talk to them. The TY students commanded all of the attention. The brothers decided to divide and conquer. One of them worked/interacted with the students, while the other stayed closer to the stand and tried to talk to the teachers, who hovered nearby.

3. Wording/explaining your product

Because they were saying things repeatedly, they kept an eye on each other to make sure the message was always clear, sounded fresh and that they were selling in the best possible way. They were conscious that it can be difficult, at the end of

171

the day, when you have done it hundreds of times, to make your answers to questions sound as fresh as they did when you received your first enquiry – but that is what you must do.

They also quibbled continuously over wording. They critiqued each other all the time trying to find a better way to say something, a quicker way, a clearer way to explain. They were conscious that they needed to have a clear selling message (a business elevator pitch), but that they also had to be open to having a bit of craic with people as well.

4. Respect other exhibitors

They were conscious that they needed to respect the other exhibitors. After all, everyone had paid money for a stand, and they were attracting a lot of attention and possibly making more noise than the others. So they worked with the other exhibitors, for example, the Order of Malta who had a stand directly opposite them. Several times they went over to the Order's stand and had one of their puppets resuscitate the dummy so that the students were drawn to that stand while still experiencing interaction from the High Rock team.

5. Learn from the other exhibitors

They also tried to speak with as many other exhibitors as possible. They do not believe that they are all competitors. As they are all part of an industry that is providing services to transition-year students, the other exhibitors were probably experiencing the same problems as they were and looking for similar solutions. The brothers believed that it was simply good common sense to talk to others and see how they were finding the business of selling into the TY school sector.

6. Target audience

The audience at the exhibition was a mix of teachers and students, which they felt probably didn't work. Students don't book the gigs, their teachers do. They felt that the organisers needed to review their audience and establish who exactly they were targeting going forward. If it was a student audience, then they would need a series of entertainments. If it was an audience of teachers, they would need information about TY options, costs, availability, etc.

7. Lead generation and new business

They received a lot of interest and some enquiries, but not as much business (confirmed bookings) from the exhibition as they had expected. However, they know that new courses can be slow burners. Sometimes teachers mightn't come back to you for a few years until they are in another school perhaps, or when there is more money available, or it might be that they are new to the role and reluctant to commit to anything new in their first year in the job.

Would they do it again? The simple answer is yes. They are both supporters of the TY Expo. They think it is a very good idea and will support it into the future, but they believe that the audience needs to be refined.

9

CONFERENCES

Everyone who runs a business attends conferences and seminars. We mostly go to seminars in order to find out more about a particular item in detail. For conferences, we attend so that we can hear keynote speakers and be inspired by them. And of course, we also attend both because they provide great networking opportunities.

Attending a conference as an individual on behalf of your business does not provide you with opportunities to put a focus on your business. Rather, it gives you an opportunity to learn and do some good networking. You might develop new contacts and come away with new ideas about how to approach things, but the main body of people attending the conference will not know that you have been there.

If you are a keynote speaker at a conference, or sponsor a conference, that is entirely different. Sponsoring a conference means that your business is associated with the industry, the speakers and the event. Your brand will be closely associated with the conference, which enhances your visibility and also 'positions' you as a key player in your industry. If you create the conference that you sponsor you will, of course, be involved in all of the organisation. If, however, you sponsor an existing conference, you pay a fee to the organisers and get all of the benefits without having to do any of the organising.

BECOMING A SPEAKER

Conferences are usually industry specific. They are geared to the financial industry, PR industry, retail industry or whatever. If it is an audience that you want to be known and respected in, you should consider offering yourself as a keynote speaker.

How do you go about it? Well let's look at the steps involved.

The most important point here is that you are a good speaker. If you are not, you should not volunteer. There is no point in giving people an opportunity to have a negative experience of your business. You might be better to put forward a colleague to speak on behalf of the business instead, or you might begin by getting some training. It is said that public speaking is one of the great stresses that people have. It is up there with death and moving house! If you are stressed by the idea of addressing a large group of people you need to ask yourself, in the first instance, if this is something that you want or need to learn to overcome.

Will it be necessary for you to speak publicly more often in the future? If it will, then you should learn the skill. If it will not, then you can decide if you want to learn, or if you want to find someone to delegate to.

Structuring a presentation for a conference works to certain rules. You will need to have a PowerPoint or Prezi presentation prepared. People expect to have something to look at while you are speaking. Your presentation should be visual – not a lot of text that you can read from the screen (the audience can do that themselves). You might need to involve some colleagues in preparing the visuals for you. If you know what you are speaking about, and have an outline of the speech, pass the project to a colleague to create clever visuals for you!

Your speech will be divided into three parts – beginning, middle and end. You will work to the established formula – tell them what you are going to tell them, tell them, then tell them what you have just told them. People are listening to learn. Give them something useful to take away from your talk.

People are also listening to be entertained. Learning should never be dull. A genius who cannot present is an opportunity lost to that audience. We have little patience if we are asked to sit through a poor speaker, or listen to a poorly structured presentation. Our time is precious. We will probably not blame the speaker (it's not the poor divil's fault that they cannot present), but we will blame the organisers for asking them to do so (and forcing us to witness it). Remember how ruthless you are at conferences? People will be the same when you are speaking.

If you are offering yourself as a speaker, you believe that you know something of interest to the audience. You need to establish exactly what that is. You might know a lot about education, but every one of your peers attending an education conference will know a lot too. *What will make your presentation different?* Have you conducted research into the future of third-level education for example? Can you reveal findings about the kind of jobs that will require a master's degree at entry level in the future? Do you have expertise in comparing education systems around the world? Can you speak about trends in other countries or on other continents which might impact the Irish education system? Have you written a book about a specific area of education and would you like to share your insights into the subject (you might also have the book on sale at the same time)? If you are as 'generally' knowledgeable as everyone else attending then you have no reason to be a speaker. Find an expertise and sharpen it.

You then need to start learning the craft of the speaker. Look at speakers you admire. Why are they so good? They make it look very easy don't they? That's because they put a lot of work into making sure that their presentations are fully researched, rehearsed and relevant to the audience. I once interviewed Elizabeth Tierney, who wrote a book about the art of good presentation. She told me about a conference she was attending where she sneaked into the hall before the opening of the event and saw the keynote speaker walking the stage, checking the space, listening for creaking floorboards, checking the sound levels from the microphones, etc., in advance of his presentation. She was amazed, as the speaker was Sir Anthony O'Reilly, a well-known businessman who had been giving speeches for forty or fifty years. She was delighted to find that he prepared for every speech as if it were his first.

Be careful if you are using technology. The simplest piece of technology can let you down. I usually ask people to make sure that my PowerPoint presentation has been set up before I arrive to prevent any mishaps on the day (I am not good at finding technical solutions to problems!). In 2014 I was speaking at the first ever Event Management Conference in Abuja, Nigeria. The night before, I called into the hall to check that my presentation had been uploaded and because I could rehearse in an almost empty hall. As it transpired, the visuals in the presentation looked entirely wrong and out of focus on a big screen. I had checked them, and so had my colleagues, in advance of sending them to Nigeria. Checking in advance meant that a colleague could spend some time that evening correcting the PowerPoint so that the audience would have a good visual as well as aural experience the next day.

Remember, too, that you speak more quickly when you are nervous, and public speaking is always something you should be mildly nervous about. Moreover, you will naturally pick up more pace as you proceed and Irish people tend to speak quickly anyway, so if you speed it up, it becomes very difficult for anyone to understand you. And in case you are wondering, this does not only apply to those for whom English is not their first language. I gave a presentation in Dublin some time ago and afterwards a Welsh couple came up to me and told me they had difficulty following everything I had said! Deliberately slow down, and speak as clearly as you can.

If you are preparing a speech, you might be better to prepare the entire speech – word for word – and then reduce it to key points and visuals when you know exactly what you are saying. If possible, have someone in the office review the speech to highlight anything that confuses them. If it confuses on paper, it will definitely confuse when spoken! It doesn't take a lot of time to sort out these 'blimps' in advance, but it will make a lot of difference to the audience's experience of your speech.

Practise your speech. I'm not really a fan of practising in front of a mirror (I get too distracted with my facial expressions or the movement of my hands), but I am a big fan of rehearsing every word that you are going to say. You can do this in the car travelling to and from meetings, you can do it while you are gardening at the weekend or walking the dog. Make sure that you have all of the information clear in your head before you enter the hall to stand and speak.

Do not use the conference as an opportunity to plug your business. People did not come to hear you advertise. Share your expertise with them and they will associate that level of knowledge with your business anyway.

Be open to questions and answers at the end and expect that someone might ask you something that you cannot answer. It happens. You are there as an expert speaker, not as a seer! If you cannot answer a question, offer to find out and let the organisers know so that they can share the response with attendees – and thank the person for asking such a clever question!

Finally, learn from the feedback that people give you. One of the first speeches I ever made was in a community hall in central Dublin. A lady came up to me afterwards and said that while I was good she found it really annoying looking for my neck. I asked her to explain, as her comment didn't make sense to me. She said that as soon as I started to speak, I hunched my shoulders so that they rose to the height of my chin and my neck couldn't be seen! For many months afterwards I began every speech thinking 'I hope they can see my neck'!

CREATING A CONFERENCE

The other option open to you is to create or sponsor a conference in your industry. This means that the entire conference is branded with your company name and people associate the event with you. You are, immediately, seen as an industry leader. I am talking about Irish conferences here – international conferences are a different creature altogether.

Organising a conference involves a lot of steps. First, you need to decide what time of the year will be most appropriate. You know your industry. When is the 'quiet' time that people will actually be able to attend?

Then you need to look at a location. Where is most of the industry based? Is it Dublin centred? Or Belfast/ Cork/Galway? Or is it nationwide? This will determine where you choose to have your conference. It might suit everyone travelling to attend if the conference is in Athlone, or it might be preferable to have the conference in Dublin because many speakers will be flying in to attend. Location is important because it also says something about expectation. If you have a five-star hotel as the venue for your conference, people will expect a five-star conference.

Once you decide on the venue, you need to figure out

how long the conference will run for. Should you start with a single day conference? If so, would it be better to get all of the delegates together the night before for an informal evening of networking? Or should you have a dinner on the evening of the conference? What time should you finish to allow guests to catch buses/trains/planes to get back to work the following day?

If you are organising a networking evening on the night before the event, will you do wine and finger food only? Who will welcome everyone and encourage them to network as much as possible? Or will you host a dinner just for the speakers the night before? Speakers like to have an opportunity to meet each other before they share a podium. Your MC for the event will also thank you for having an opportunity to learn something about the personalities of the speakers, which will help them with the introduction the next day.

You will need to select and book the speakers. Before you can do this, you need an idea of the topics that you are planning to cover and the running order of the event. Most conferences will have two to three speakers per session who will often stay on the platform and form a panel to answer audience questions afterwards. Each of these three speakers will be addressing a specific topic – the use of colouring agents in foods, for example – but each will need to address the issue from a different perspective. For example, one might deal with the science involved, another might deal with the popularity of different colours for different age groups, and a third might talk about future trends which are likely to impact on the industry. You will need to brief each of them about the topic you want them to cover.

I had a speaker at a conference some years ago and, at the dinner the night before, each of the group was talking about their subject for the following day. One speaker said that he would be talking about himself and his life experiences generally (he was very well known). When the meal was over, I walked him to the lift in the hotel and gently mentioned that he was mistaken about the topic that he was covering (I was embarrassed that he would get it wrong). I had not anticipated his answer, however! He said that he never paid much attention to what people asked him to speak about because he was a very entertaining speaker and people always loved him! I was blown away by his arrogance, so I gently told him that I didn't mind what he spoke about at all, I was sure that he would be wonderful, but – just for clarity – if he did not speak about the brief he had been given he would not be paid. Incredibly, he found himself capable of speaking 'on topic' the next day!

Some speakers will be known to you, will be based in Ireland and will be happy to speak for a small fee.

Others will be sourced externally. You should check speakers' agencies in Ireland and the UK (possibly in the USA) for speakers who will enhance your conference and communicate with authority on a particular area. However, they will be more expensive.

When choosing speakers it is best if you can either see a video of them in action, or look in on a streaming session that they are speaking at. You are looking for knowledge and delivery – both are equally important. Look also at the costs of speakers. Those in the public eye are often more expensive than the academics who know more. However, those in the public eye attract the attention – your job is to balance both requirements.

If you are booking speakers you will also need to pay for their travel and accommodation. Be careful about things like the mini-bar (specifically state if it is excluded) and any additional charges to the room, etc. You would be amazed sometimes at how little people expect to pay for themselves.

Each speaker should be able to provide you with a biography for your conference brochure and their speech or PowerPoint presentation in advance. The biography will be used, with a photograph, in the printed material that you issue about the conference when people are booking. The speech or PowerPoint printout can be included in the delegates' pack on the day.

If yours is a two-day conference, you will need to organise a dinner on the night of the first evening. Plan it carefully. Delegates and speakers will probably be staying overnight. If they are all business people they will appreciate a
good meal, a witty after-dinner speaker and an opportunity
to network. After-dinner speakers are very popular, but they
need to be well known (they could be sportspeople, former
politicians, television personalities). This allows the attendees to get an enjoyable insight into their lives. They must
also be able to combine an element of learning (they might
be powerful 'encouraging' speakers who will leave their
audience inspired and invigorated) and should be witty.

Be very careful about speakers' humour. It can go
terribly wrong. What is regarded as funny by a group of
people who know each other, can be decidedly un-funny to
a group of business colleagues. What can be entertaining
to a group of all men or all women can be offensive to
a mixed group. Carefully check the 'humour' of your
speaker. I once attended a business dinner where the
keynote speaker – very well known and highly regarded
– gave an excellent speech, which was thoroughly enjoyed
by the audience. Then he ended with a slightly tongue-in-
cheek, mildly off-colour, 'funny' story, which managed to
be ageist and sexist at the same time, and caused confusion
to the international audience who didn't understand the
punchline. No one was happy at the end!

Entertainment for this group is also an issue. They will not be inclined to 'dance till dawn' so you will need to provide either a floor show for them (so that they can sit and be entertained) or background music so that they can continue networking.

You have numerous other decisions to take as well. Will you begin with breakfast networking the second morning? Or will you allow delegates to eat breakfast and then attend the conference? How much will you charge? Are you planning to recover all of the costs or will you charge what seems to be a reasonable fee for the event and part-sponsor some element yourself. Will you encourage others to co-sponsor? Could you involve a printer for example? Would sponsorship from a newspaper be appropriate?

Who will open the conference? Can you get a minister, who will bring a certain gravitas to the event, to perform that function? If so, who will meet and greet the minister? How will they be introduced? What will the minister be expected to talk about? Will you offer to provide a briefing document for the civil servants? How long will the minister be able to stay? What kind of publicity can you get from their attendance? Are you booking a photographer and/or a videographer for the event? Will you try to capture key moments on video – possibly so that you can create a visual montage of speakers' key moments, which you might use for the promotion of next year's events? Will you have a photographer on hand to get photographs of the minister, the keynote speakers and the attendees so that you can issue them to traditional and new media during or after the event? Have you invited any tweeters to attend? Will you be encouraging the conference attendees to tweet throughout? Are you trying to have your conference trending on the day? If you are bringing over someone very well known, can you get them interviewed on *The Late Late Show* or *The Saturday Night Show*? Television exposure might encourage more people to attend the conference, and it will certainly encourage your clients and audience to see your business in a different light.

What will the pack that the attendees receive on arrival contain? Will you provide name badges, copies of speeches, biographies of the speakers, and information about your business and why you are sponsoring the event? Will you have an exhibition area during the event? Will you encourage people to take an exhibition space and promote their goods to those attending? How much will you charge for this? Will you bring in an exhibition company to organise this element for you? Can you arrange to have coffee breaks taken in the exhibition area so that you are driving traffic to those stands? Will you have a stand yourselves?

If the hotel is a distance outside of town, can you arrange for people to be collected at a central location like the train or bus station? Can you provide buses to ferry them to and from their locations? Will you have the dinner in the same hotel as the conference, or will you bring people to another location – a distillery, jail or castle – for their evening meal? If you go down this route, you are responsible for creating and maintaining the atmosphere throughout.

And after all this organisation, how will you evaluate the success of this venture? Will you conduct surveys among those attending to ask them to rate the level of satisfaction with each individual speaker? Will you also rate the organisers, the hotel accommodation, the food, the friendliness of the staff? And, almost as important, will you listen to the feedback that you receive?

At the height of the recession, I addressed an industry conference. The speaker before me was a wildly optimistic, highly charged, super-active speaker who believed that as long as you looked upon the glass as being rosy, it probably was. My presentation followed (about how to promote a business in an economic crisis) and we then all took coffee together. Many of the delegates mentioned the first speaker and how annoying they found him. He wasn't living in the real world was the overall impression. I mentioned that this feedback should be given to the organisers for future years. The delegates I spoke with said that this had been done the previous year but nobody had listened, obviously, as the speaker had been invited again the next year!

If you are planning an annual event, then it is vital that you learn from your mistakes and listen to feedback, so you can present the best conference possible, encouraging delegates to return year after year and showing that you are the best at what you do. This good publicity will only reflect well on your business dealings in general.

CASE STUDY – AN INTERNATIONAL CONFERENCE

This case study is based on an interview with Seamus McCann from Consulting Ireland.

For most new businesses, conferences mean an opportunity to attend and learn, or possibly to sponsor. For one organisation – Consulting Ireland – a conference presented an opportunity to showcase themselves, their members and the country.

Consulting Ireland was formed in 2010, to identify international business opportunities for Irish companies and organisations, particularly in emerging markets (Africa, South and Eastern Europe, South America and the Middle East). The organisation focuses on the IFI (International Financing Institutions) market and seeks projects that are funded by, for example, The World Bank. It started as an initiative of Enterprise Ireland, which approached Seamus McCann and some others and invited them to an initial meeting. Enterprise Ireland wanted an initiative that was driven by the private sector, so they encouraged them to form an association. Consulting Ireland was the result.

The first step was to create a web portal with a small amount of funding from Enterprise Ireland. Then seminars were held around the country to inform businesses about the size of the market and the opportunities available, and to give them information about how to enter the market. These seminars were free; the first was held in Limerick in late 2010.

From a business perspective, going after markets funded by the World Bank, for example, makes sense. The business is guaranteed payment, and there is a safety factor too, with the possibility of getting up to 60 per cent funding in advance. Membership is open to everyone, from one- to two-person businesses to major international companies like HP and Microsoft.

Arising from these seminars, Enterprise Ireland invited the organisation to apply for cluster funding for mentoring. Consulting Ireland raised half the money and these funds were matched by Enterprise Ireland. Forty companies participated in a nine-month-long training programme in 2013–2014. The programme not only taught them how to go through the tender process for the IFI market, but it actually assisted them in tendering and putting in expressions of interest.

In addition to the work they were doing in Ireland, Consulting Ireland began reaching out to other organisations sponsored by regional governments, and started to make presentations to them. They got into discussion with the region of Alsace and decided to promote greater cooperation between companies in Alsace and Ireland. The Alsace region, and Strasbourg in particular, offered a door into France and French-speaking West Africa. In addition, Consulting Ireland also began working closely with the Catalan regional government, which opened doors to Barcelona, Spain and the wider Latin-American market. They also identified a need for a non-EU member state to be involved with their organisation, so they approached the Agder region in southern Norway, which soon became involved.

All of these are very progressive regions. France and Ireland had the idea of setting up a group called IFI Global. The Spanish had the idea that representatives should meet face-to-face. The result was the first IFI global networking opportunity, held in 2013. It was a small event: four Irish companies, three to four French companies and ten Spanish companies took part. It was held over a single day and offered companies an opportunity to identify potential partners in other regions.

Arising from the success of that meeting, it was agreed that it should be done again. This time most partners agreed that it should be organised by Ireland. Consulting Ireland is the only member of the group which represents a country: the others represent regions. In addition, Ireland is an English-speaking country and the majority of tenders are presented in English. As Consulting Ireland wanted to be the administrative hub for the new grouping, there were no objections from Seamus.

With about a year's notice, the organisation decided to take the task on, but do it on a grander scale if possible. A committee of six to eight Irish people was formed to organise it. Their first decision was that they would expand the event from a networking meeting to a conference.

Then they had to identify the audience they were targeting. They had two different types of companies in mind. The first was new companies who had never worked in this area before.

The object was to inform and educate them about the World Bank and the IFI market in general. The second was more experienced companies which didn't need the information (the French and Spanish companies that were already IFI-savvy companies), but would benefit from making business contacts who could co-tender with them for projects.

The committee agreed that they would need at least 100 participants to break even (in the end, they had 153 delegates). The French companies paid a fee, as they had previously received free seminars at the IFI meeting in 2013. Despite this, the French were very enthusiastic about attending. However, the organisers felt that a little extra incentive was needed for the Spanish, so they did not charge them to attend the event. The commitment to pay their own fares and accommodation was sufficient. As a result, the Catalonian companies were also well represented at the conference, and the group has now extended invitations to the Valencian and Andalucían regions to join.

The choice of venue was more difficult than the organisers had anticipated. They wanted to house all of the participants under one roof and originally wanted a city centre hotel. However, they could not find one with the available capacity for the time of the conference. Instead, they decided to host the conference at City West Hotel. Initially, they were worried that delegates might want to be closer to the city, but in the end they felt that the location worked to their advantage by keeping all of the participants together without any external distractions. They all got to know each other better in the bars and restaurants of the hotel, outside of conference time, which might not have happened if there had been city centre distractions on their doorsteps.

Minister Richard Bruton was chosen as the perfect person to open the conference. This issue was an important one – the conference was organised for companies from all over Ireland and they wanted to show that the government took this area of business seriously. Luckily their committee had good links in many areas, including with PR consultancies working with the government, and Minister Bruton did, indeed, open the conference.

The organisers also had to develop the programme for the conference. They decided to invite speakers from the main IFIs like the World Bank, the European Bank for Reconstruction and Development and the Asian Development Bank. This hadn't been done before. These organisations responded positively when they were invited, as they were attracted by the idea of speaking to an international audience. It was, in fact, much harder to get speakers from Ireland!

As well as this, it was decided that each of the partner regions would chair a different session of the conference. This was important, as they wanted everyone to feel included in the event. For the very first session, they chose speakers from Spain, France and Ireland. These speakers were from carefully chosen, successful companies that had positive experiences of tendering for international contracts. All were small companies and, in the case of the Irish speakers, all had participated in the earlier networking opportunity. All of the Irish speakers were novices and, as it happened, they were all from the IT sector, but that was purely coincidental.

The organisers gave companies the option of bringing pull-ups or banners with them, if they wanted, and displaying them in the main conference hall, at no cost. They also hired a large meeting room outside of the main conference room, which was mainly used by the French for one-to-one meetings with potential partners. Every participant completed profile information and all of the profiles were made available to the participants before the conference. The French had identified specific companies that they wanted to talk to, before they even arrived in Ireland. However, with hindsight, the organising committee felt that they probably should have planned to have an exhibition hall. They were even approached by a UK company who offered to run an exhibition at the event, at no cost to the organisers. However, in the end, the UK company couldn't get up the interest, so the idea fell by the wayside.

Originally there was an idea that parallel sessions could be organised, but this was decided against in the end because of the size of the audience. It was felt that this was the right decision to make, not to divide the group.

The conference was one and a half days long. The organisers felt that one day was too little for companies travelling from

France and Spain, as it would be difficult to justify the cost and the organisation, but one and a half days seemed ideal. On the afternoon of the second day, which was free, the committee offered to arrange a tour of Dublin if the delegates were interested. No one took them up on this. The French went off to meet their ambassador and do some sightseeing. The Spanish went their own way and attended other pre-arranged business meetings. The Norwegians went home. Curiously, the Norwegians brought a business journalist with them to write about the event and see what exactly was going on. Norway will host the conference in 2016 and had already begun planning it before they arrived in Dublin.

The conference received some support from Enterprise Ireland and small sponsorships of €500–€1,000, but it was generally self-funding. On the evening of the first day, a meal with wine and some entertainment for the guests was provided. The evening event was to showcase Irish culture, Irish food and traditional music, singing and dancing. The craic continued in the bar afterwards. The only additional expense for delegates was that they were required to purchase their own lunch on the first day of the conference. No one even commented on this.

In terms of lessons learned, the organisers say that there were many – and a lot relate to time:

- They should have started organising the conference much earlier.

- They felt that they didn't identify the theme fast enough.

- Speakers and topics were a bit last minute (because of the late selection of the theme).

- They didn't have specific topics for each speaker and felt they should have given them a better briefing about the areas they wanted them to cover.

- They could have been better on the promotion side, but they were hampered by the fact that the PR person on the team became ill.

- The sub-committee worked very well together, but they had to rely too much on the committee (putting huge pressure on a small number of individuals).

- In the final three months before the conference, Consulting Ireland took on an administrator who looked after the day-to-day issues. This was an expense that they had not factored into their costings.

- If they were doing it again in the future, and they had some money, they might bring in an event organiser.

On the plus side:

- Consulting Ireland received a lot of recognition by government bodies for the work they are doing.

- The organisation is now better known by Irish companies.

- They proved that there is a market out there and a genuine interest to participate in it.

- They received good support from the World Bank and other IFI organisations, which bodes well for the future and ongoing initiatives.

- The conference was a great success.

10

SOCIAL MEDIA

When radio first arrived, people said that it heralded the death of newspapers. Then television was supposed to replace radio. Social media was supposed to replace them all. So what actually happened?

Each time a new form of communication is found we add it to the other forms already in existence and, as business people, seek to use all of them to reach our customers. Social media has enhanced the way we communicate with one another and created new opportunities for communication, information and explanation. As it has progressed it has become more visual. It is also highly interactive. It requires a lesser amount of depth and a greater speed of delivery. Social media is different and should be treated differently.

So why bother at all? Well, unless your business has closed, you will have customers who seek their information from social media. If your customers are there, you should be there too.

Who uses social media? Surprisingly, just about everyone. It is not confined to younger people (although they are the biggest category of users), it is not confined to the developed world (the developing world has high levels of social media interaction, even though their Internet access may be poor) and it is not used to the same extent by all users. Let's look at it in a little more detail.

Social media means that people can now be in touch with each other all the time. The growth of tools like WhatsApp, Snapchat and even the humble text message means that people are in constant contact with friends and colleagues. Information is packaged in smaller parcels, is communicated more frequently than the old telephones or letters allowed for, and constant communication is a given.

People are also accessing news – world news, sports, arts information, etc. – on a constant basis. Dedicated apps on their phones bring information to their screens as it happens. Twitter allows people to keep in touch with the news and to pass it on. (When broadcaster Gerry Ryan of RTÉ died, the information was first released to the public via a tweet from Miriam O'Callaghan.)

The invention of the Internet – and the creation of Google – means that people can now access just about any information they want, at any time of the day, from several sources. Can you imagine anyone going door-to-door nowadays selling *Encyclopaedia Britannica*? The appeal in the 1960s/1970s was that you had a store of knowledge in your home for both yourselves and your family. Now everyone with a smartphone has a store of knowledge. Just type a keyword into a Google search bar and see how many hundreds or thousands of references to your item you can find, instantly.

Facebook has created a world of interaction where people's lives have moved from private to public spaces. There is a desire now to share what you are doing with the world, and to encourage the world to comment on it. Pinterest has created a community of interest which is open to all. Find your topic and, if it is even mildly visual, there will be Pinterest boards with photos, suggestions and notes about it. And how on earth did we all survive without YouTube? If you missed something, you can virtually guarantee that there is a YouTube clip of footage about it. A natural disaster, an embarrassing moment, a way to fix something that you have broken – you can find a video for that on YouTube.

In the business world, LinkedIn keeps us in touch with people who are like us. People also hang out in Google circles and bloggers are famous for sharing their thoughts with the world at large.

Welcome to the world of social media. As a business person you need to embrace it and start using it to communicate with your clients. Let's look at how you might use each of these resources in turn.

We'll begin with the simple email, which is often overlooked. Do you have a 'signature' created for everyone who responds from your business? One of my pet hates is receiving emails from Bligs and Co. without a name. It doesn't matter if someone actually typed the answer or if you received an auto-response. No person's name was given. Instead the response was anonymous. It was from 'the company'. Create signatures for all of your people so that the customer knows who they are dealing with.

Do you have rules around emails? In my business we have some very simple rules. For example, because we deal with multiple countries and many nationalities, we try to be culturally aware when we are responding. Dear is a much more acceptable form of greeting to an Asian person than Hi. Hey is perfectly acceptable in the States. Those kinds of small things matter. Also, you should have a rule that says that if someone writes to you as Ms or Mr, you respond in the same way. Hi is not an acceptable response to Dear Ms Gunning. Also, as a general rule, Hi is fine if you are mailing everyone who entered a competition that you ran, but if you respond to a query that I sent with just Hi, I'll be quite annoyed that you couldn't manage to put 'Ellen' after the greeting!

Email is instant. People expect a response almost as soon as they have sent it. Do you have a policy on how long a person will have to wait? If you get a large volume of email queries, maybe you should look at installing an auto-responder that says 'emails will be responded to within forty-eight hours max', or something along those lines.

I know that large companies will tell you that there are systems for finding keywords in emails which will allow you to respond without the intervention of a human being. It would be a great case study or piece of research for someone. How often have you received a response from an auto-responder that answered your query? In my case it has never happened. I have inevitably received a response that says check out this FAQ (frequently asked question) and if it doesn't answer your query, send us back an email with this identifying number. I'm not sure that this is acceptable for a large company, but I can understand it. It is, however, indefensible for a smaller business.

And what about the humble website? When people first put up a page on the web, it was just that. A page, a presence, and in many cases, it was treated almost like a paper book. It was there and wouldn't be changed for years. Today, however, many people begin their search for things on the web. They might call to your store to check the quality, or feel the weight, or try something on before they buy – but a lot of them have already selected your product online and you knew nothing about it.

Websites are like old-fashioned shops in some ways.

They are a window which is open onto the world displaying your products. But they are more than that. You have to imagine that the shop is actually open and people can have a 'snoop around'. They can open drawers and see if you have a bigger selection of items than are on show in the window. They can have a look at the staff area and be impressed or unimpressed by how well you treat your people. They can have a snoop at your pricing policies and check online forums to see if you are buying goods from developing countries which might have been made by children. They can have a quick look at the shop next door and see if they have a better selection or if their prices are better or if their staff are friendlier – and you will never know that they have been there. They can also, of course, decide that they really do like what you are selling and buy it – online – even though it is past midnight. Spooky isn't it?

Websites nowadays are selling tools. They are not static items. They need to be constantly revived and refreshed. You need to be putting information up on a regular basis so that people have a reason to return to the site. I once saw a demonstration of a piece of software which can show you where on your website people are looking, where their mouse travels in order to find the link (i.e., the places where they think the information SHOULD be) and therefore which parts of your website you need to put your most important information on. It was utterly fascinating. You need to make it easy for people to look around your site and find what they are looking for.

Really good web designers will tell you that it is all about clicks. How many clicks does it take to find an item on your website? If it is too many, the customer will lose interest. Just like going into a shop, if someone tells you that you need to take the lift to the second floor, walk through the menswear and past the TV sections until you reach the end of the corridor, and then climb the stairs to find something, you might not bother.

Creating a website is expensive. Expertise doesn't come cheap. Getting it wrong, however, is twice as expensive. Your site should look modern, use good photos and contain videos if possible. People like moving pictures. It should have all of the information that someone needs to help them make a purchase – is the item in stock, what size is it, how much does it cost, what is it made of, how long will it take to deliver it, is there anything else I should know about it, where can I buy? These are all basic questions which your website should be able to answer. In addition though, you should have testimonials from customers. Here are people just like the customer who have bought the same items and were very happy with the product and the service they received. It is good for other customers to be able to read their messages and see what they said! In addition, your site should have a blog. What would I like to learn about your business? Can I pick up any hints and tips from you? Are you experts in your field? Impress me with your knowledge before I buy from you. Your site might also have a news section – press releases and photographs of new business ventures that you have entered into, new countries and counties stocking your product, awards that you have won, speaking engagements that you have fulfilled, famous people you have met ... Anything and everything extra that might impress the potential costumer and encourage them to buy from you. The rules are simple and clear.

Your site should also have links to your other social media platforms. People like to go from the web to Facebook and onto your Pinterest page and generally float around your particular area of cyberspace, see what you are like and what others think of you. It is important that you get them all right.

Facebook is a different creature entirely. If someone is checking you out on Facebook, they might be looking for competitions, or pictures of others interacting with your product or company. Facebook is less serious and more interactive than your website. People 'like' your posts if they think the information is of interest, or witty, or useful. They like your page if they want to keep in touch with you and the information you post. You have 'friends' on Facebook.

The rules of Facebook interaction are very different to your website. Facebook is all about presenting the personality of the business. People will keep in touch with you because they like the fact that you do slightly wacky things perhaps, or you are always posting quirky pictures of people who work with you doing silly things in the office, or you 'get' what they are interested in and often put up links to videos or articles that they might not have seen but would be interested in reading. They might keep in touch with you because you create clever infographics or just seem human!! Facebook is that strange mix of corporate and personal. People prefer to interact with people so Facebook, in my opinion, works well if one person in the business is responsible for the postings. This means that there is a consistency of style and interest.

You will need to write the brief of course. It is your company. Your corporate image. You need to be all over it. But you can't monitor every sentence and it shouldn't need your approval for someone to reply to a post or post something to your timeline. So, you need to clearly outline your company policy for dealing with negative comments, familiarity, spell-checking responses, use of humour, etc. One of the toughest jobs is finding the right person to look after your social media for you. There are people who really enjoy social media interaction, but they also have to understand that this is costing your business money and you need to at least try to get a return from it. Finding someone who 'gets' the corporate end of things is the challenge. I'm talking about regular postings on your Facebook page. The rule seems to be that if you are not posting twice a day you are pretty much wasting your time. You can schedule in advance, by the way, so it doesn't need someone to physically be present at 9.30 a.m. or 2 p.m. each day. You can schedule a week in advance – but you should also allow space to add 'extra' posts if something of interest happens. On Facebook, the challenge is to build followers who are interested in what you do – and keep building.

LinkedIn is an amazing resource. It allows you to connect with people who keep their profiles up to date, so you always know what they are doing. It also allows you to find people you are interested in connecting with, or find a link-person who can introduce you. It allows you to create and join groups, and, of course, you can keep up to date with people and the positions they hold in business (this is probably LinkedIn's greatest plus). LinkedIn is a great source of knowledge too. People like to help people answer questions. They will give you feedback if you look for it. They won't mind if you reach out to them to ask for assistance.

I was in the bank the other day. It has those double doors as you enter – the ones where the first door must be fully closed before the second door opens. The first door was almost closed when I arrived. I opened it and stepped inside. 'Sorry,' I said to the guy in front me, 'you'd swear I had to wait for hours for it to open again wouldn't you? I've no patience.'

'No worries,' he said. 'Are you Ellen Gunning?'

Well, I was quite sure that I had never laid eyes on him before. 'I am,' I said. 'How do I know you?'

'We're connected on LinkedIn,' he replied. 'You're very active aren't you? I recognised you from your photo.'

If you ever wanted proof that social media interaction works – there it is!

Twitter is used by a different category of people again. It is very popular with journalists and my impression is that Twitter is used by mid-thirties to mid-fifties people. It requires you to reduce the information you are sending to 140 characters – short, sharp bursts of information. Twitter uses hashtags so that you can easily identify the topic, or add other people or businesses into the conversation. Twitter is 'instant'. People respond immediately. They re-tweet your messages to their followers. This means that your message can get beyond the, say, 2,000 followers that you have and reach 200,000 people via re-tweets. Unlike Facebook, tweeters thank each other and re-tweet information about themselves. So, if your business tweeted that you loved the new advertising campaign from a well-known designer, you could expect that the designer will re-tweet that comment to their followers. It's a bit like saying – look, other people think we are doing a good job!

Remember that you can also schedule Twitter. In fact you can use something like Hootsuite to schedule posts which will issue on Twitter and Facebook at the same time. Technology can help to save you some time on this one.

YouTube is an entirely different phenomenon and one that you can use in a number of different ways. YouTube is testament to the power of video. People love to watch videos. You can create videos for your own business and put them on YouTube and then link them to your website. This is actually a good way of doing it (some regard it as better than loading the video onto your site). YouTube videos vary in quality – some are very well made, with great production values; they've had a lot of money spent on them. Others are produced much more cheaply. They are all, generally, short and highly visual. YouTube allows you to create videos with a hand-held camera if you want. You do not have to spend a fortune (although as a corporate I think you should always have your video professionally produced for you).

You can create your own channel on YouTube and put all of your videos up there. Let's assume that you are a kitchen manufacturer. Look at the opportunities that YouTube will give you. It will allow you to put up a corporate video that tells everyone about your business, how it got started, what kinds of kitchens you produce, who has bought from you in the past. You can also create videos which show the latest trends in kitchens – are big silver fridges still the thing? What about disguising dishwashers – is that still popular? Are people still into hanging their cooking implements from hooks in the ceiling? What's the trend in relation to hobs in the middle of the kitchen on a free-standing pedestal?

You could also do videos that show the quality of your craftsmanship. Instead of telling people that your work is of a high standard, shoot a video which shows the drawers opening and closing, effortlessly, a few hundred times!! Or shoot a video showing how someone in your showroom creates that drawer unit. Or shoot a video showing before and after – old house with old kitchen/ripped out/new kitchen fitted. Videos don't require people to use their imaginations – text does! Make it easy for them to see how you create your cabinets. This in turn makes it easier for them to understand the quality of your work or the value of your craftsmanship.

Pinterest is a platform for primarily stills photography and is really good if your product or business lends itself easily to photos. For instance, Pinterest is terrific if you are an interior designer. You could 'pin' samples of materials that you will be using on upholstery in the coming year. You could pin new colours for the autumn, or designs that you have created for customers. You could 'pin' before and after photos, or instructions on how to cover an armchair.

Then there is Google+. I once asked a colleague if my business should be pinning to Google+, putting up videos and still photos, encouraging people to hang out with us in our Google circles. 'How effective is it?' I asked.

'What is the word in front of the plus?' he asked. 'If Google have created it, they will "find" information there for their search engines. Of course you should be using it!'

There are some great advantages to using social media. The first is that you control the message. It is not mediated by anyone. It is not 'interpreted' by the media, it is 'remembered' and shared by someone. It is your message, using the visuals and the language you have chosen, distributed to a large number of people. You certainly have control with social media in the same way that you have with your own print items (but which you do not have with the media, be that newspapers, radio or television).

Social media also allows you to track interaction, which is wonderful. You can check the analytics and see where people are coming from (to get to your page), what age bracket they fit into, where they live, how long they spent on your site, which pages they looked at, where they stopped, and what was the jumping-off point. It is amazing how much you can learn, which you can then use to tailor your business.

CASE STUDY – MEDIAHQ

This case study is based on an interview with Jack Murray from MediaHQ. Jack developed his business from the production of a print manual to an online service, which has a dedicated and highly structured social media strategy for promotion. His company, MediaHQ, won 'Best Marketing and Communications Blog company 2015' at the Blog Awards Ireland, sponsored by the Ashville Media Group.

Jack Murray knows about press offices. He worked in the Progressive Democrats' press office for a number of years before forming his own business. He bought the Irish media directory business from Mick Burns in 2006, and 2007 was his first full year publishing. The physical version of the directory died in 2008 – he made it obsolete.

A media directory is an important tool for anyone issuing press releases. Jack realised that they were publishing every six months and there were approximately 23,000 changes each time. A move by one journalist generally begets ten changes to the directory. Jack's company was publishing 3,000 directories each time, with a special edition for the Public Relations Institute of Ireland. It was a vital tool for the PR industry.

His business analysis told him that PR people were spending a lot of productive time doing grunt work and putting media lists together. What every consultancy needs is the gift of time, i.e. billable hours. It didn't make sense for this amount of manpower to be used in the collection and maintenance of databases. Ken Robertson, Head of Mischief at Paddy Power bookmakers, told Jack that if he put the directory online, Paddy Power would be his first customer!

He started looking for a solution and someone told him that he 'needed the cloud'. He started the MediaHQ project in 2008. He rejected the option of buying a software system from the USA and instead spent fourteen months writing cheques to feed 'the monster' to develop the site. He worked closely with a development agency and sent them seventy- to ninety-page briefing documents.

Initially Jack was looking at creating an online resource for PR people, which would provide details of journalists, their specialisations and the newspapers or magazines that they were writing for. As the project developed, he built in a facility for users to create their own mailing lists and store them on site. He added a facility to upload and distribute press releases. Now he really had a product that he could market to PR agencies.

In 2009 they turned it on. The company believes that what they are providing is not a media list option, but media intelligence. Within six months, revenue from his new online listing service had overtaken revenue from the printed book. They had a success on their hands.

The online system MediaHQ.com is used by in-house teams

and smaller agencies, but not so much by larger agencies, which are slower to change. The company employs a core team of ten, which increases to fifteen at times. They have two teams working each day, Monday to Thursday, from 9 a.m. to 11 p.m. They work hard to ensure that there is a very low level of bounces for emails (3 to 5 per 100 is the acceptable level) and to drive traffic to the stories issued by their clients, through social media.

The business uses social media extensively to develop and promote the brand. They will tweet about a story (theirs or a client's) four times in a day. The key trend in tweets at the moment is personalisation. Corporate tweets are not well regarded. The MediaHQ Twitter account lists the people who tweet on behalf of the organisation, and they use their initials when tweeting so that you know which 'real person' is communicating with you. They also monitor what other corporates are doing and try to mimic best practice, with tweets about going out for ice cream on a hot day and that kind of thing.

They use social media very effectively to support the brand, including LinkedIn. They blog a lot and spend quite a bit of time generating content. They create form content, for example a feature on three young journalists to watch for the future. They also create blogs around the lists that they build (for example, Christmas lists). They have recently started to ask guest bloggers to contribute.

Jack firmly believes that if you have a hunch about your industry you should blog about it. It's all about the headline. MediaHQ always does five tweets around a blog. They work hard to make sure that their content is shared. In fact, they plan their content six weeks in advance. Copy is always written well ahead of time. They also use Twitter, Facebook and podcasts. Their podcasts are a maximum of twenty-five minutes long and Jack uses the opportunity of travel, for example, to meet with people who might not otherwise be available to an Irish audience and interview them for a podcast.

Five people in the office work on content, two people work on marketing and the remainder of his staff work on research, web development, sales, content development, customer satisfaction and front end marketing.

Jack Murray has a world vision. He wants to build an international brand around the piece of technology which he has developed. He believes that he can capture data from any country in the world and successfully have MediaHQs all over the globe. His incredibly disciplined and strategic use of social media will get him there, well ahead of the posse.

EPILOGUE

THINK LIKE A PR PERSON

I hope that, by now, you, like me, believe in the power of communication. I honestly believe that it is vital to stay in touch with your customers, key influencers, even your competitors. You need people to be able to find you in the places that they like to search and you need to be constantly working on the different types of media. The cost of media platforms is minuscule, but you need to properly evaluate what you are doing and what return you are getting from them.

You are presumably employing a person to look after your publicity – everything from your press releases to Facebook posts, from arranging speaking opportunities for you to creating infographics for Pinterest, from organising your stands at exhibitions to creating really interesting photo call opportunities, from writing and issuing press releases to negotiating sponsorship deals, and from writing and issuing your ezines to pinning and tweeting about your achievements. It's great to have so much going on and the joined-up effect of it all is much more than the sum total of the parts. But you need to return to why you are doing it all and see if it is paying its way.

Let's look at each of the tools of the trade again in turn and the important questions you should be asking yourself about the results of each.

A press release costs very little in terms of money. There is virtually no cost of distribution. The cost is labour-related. It is the time taken to develop the angles, write and issue the release. At the end of perhaps a year, you should review your press release success rate. How many releases have been covered by the media? How much publicity did they attract? Was it in the media outlets/newspapers/magazines that you were targeting? Did others comment on the coverage to you? Did it help you to reach a wider audience, or reinforce your presence with existing customers? Was it worth the effort? Who were you targeting? Did you reach them?

In contrast, there is the potentially much more ex-pensive third-party endorsement. Did it work for you? Who did you use? How much did it cost? How often did they appear on your behalf? What kind of feedback did you get? Did you pick up additional media coverage as a result of having this person involved? What comments did people feed back to you? Was the cost justified in your opinion? Should you renew the contract with your endorser for another year? Should you seek a new contract with a different endorser? Should you grow the panel of endorsers and add a second while keeping the first? What did your target audience think of these people? Did you do research or can you do research to make sure that you get the right ones?

How much time went into organising your press receptions? How many did you hold? Who did you have present at them? How many of the invited media attended? How many media took and used photographs afterwards? Did coverage appear in the media that you were targeting? What feedback did you get from attendees and others? Who were you trying to influence? What proportion of your business comes from people who read the social pages? Did they comment on your receptions? Are they still in your customer base?

Did your photo calls show a good return? What photographer or photographers did you use? Which ones were easiest to work with? Who delivered the most creative photos? What photos were used by the media? Did you appear in the jokey 'PR pics' section of the *Sunday Independent* or in the real pages of the papers? (By the way, a lot of people look at the jokey PR photos section – if it showcases your brand you might regard it as a good thing.) How widely were you able to use these photos? Did they help to create the right impression about your company?

And what about your sponsorship? How much did it cost you? Was it a good investment? Were people talking about you? Did it change impressions or create good vibes? If you were targeting the local community, did anyone locally evaluate the impact of your sponsorship?

Your newsletter will cost you for monthly distribution as well as photographs – so be sure to check your analytics. How many people received them? How many people opened them? Which were the most popular stories? What kind of feedback did you get? How many people visited your website from your ezine?

Did you create entertainment opportunities? Who did you entertain? How much did it cost? What did you want to achieve? Was the purpose of the entertainment to keep existing clients or win new ones?

Were exhibitions that you participated in well attended? Poorly attended? Did your stand look as well as it should? Could you capture names and contact details of people who were interested in your company or your product? Can you quantify the business that you got as a direct result of your participation in that exhibition? Do you know how much business other exhibitors at the same event did? How did you compare with them?

And what about conferences and seminars? Did you organise any? Did you speak at any? How successful was your engagement? Did you win new business? Have you been invited to speak at other events? Were you successful in your endeavours?

You don't really have much option with your website, but you should look at the cost of maintaining it, the cost of photography and video production which you put on it, possibly the cost of a blogger. How many sales were made online? Did the website always look 'sharp'? The only evaluation here is whether or not your site is good enough and how much it costs to keep it looking that way. You don't have an option about having a site.

Did you create and use new social media platforms? What did you do with the Facebook page you created? How much interaction are you getting? How many friends and likes? Has it been successful? What about Pinterest? Did you have sufficient photos or graphics of good quality to pin? Did others re-pin? Has it expanded your sphere of influence? Are you using LinkedIn now to look for new business? Is your profile accurate and does it carefully represent who you are? Is the business active on Twitter? What are you tweeting about and who is re-tweeting, 'favouriting' or commenting on you?

Once you have evaluated all of this information, you will know how to move forward to successfully grow your business.

Public relations is not advertising. You will not be able

to say definitively that X invested equals Y returned, but you should be able to see greater levels of interaction with your company or your brand, and you should see whether you are either keeping your customers close or expanding your footprint in a new market.

Public relations is time-consuming. It needs patience, creativity, stamina, savvy, a small budget and a lot of time. It is a journey, not a destination. Find the right person for the job. Train them in the skills that they will need. Encourage them to be pro-active and open to new suggestions about ways in which you might communicate with your public.

Enjoy the journey – you never know where it might lead!

MERCIER PRESS

IRISH PUBLISHER - IRISH STORY

We hope you enjoyed this book.

Since 1944, Mercier Press has published books that have been critically important to Irish life and culture. Books that dealt with subjects that informed readers about Irish scholars, Irish writers, Irish history and Ireland's rich heritage.

We believe in the importance of providing accessible histories and cultural books for all readers and all who are interested in Irish cultural life.

Our website is the best place to find out more information about Mercier, our books, authors, news and the best deals on a wide variety of books. Mercier tracks the best prices for our books online and we seek to offer the best value to our customers, offering free delivery within Ireland.

Sign up on our website to receive updates and special offers.

www.mercierpress.ie
www.facebook.com/mercier.press
www.twitter.com/irishpublisher

Mercier Press, Unit 3b, Oak House, Bessboro Rd, Blackrock, Cork, Ireland